# Lord Teach Me to Pray

*Exposing the Power and Practice of Daily Prayer*

Rev. Michael K. Jones, M.Div.

**xulon**
PRESS

*Lord, Teach Me to Pray*
*Exposing the Power and Practice of Daily Prayer*
by Rev. Michael K. Jones, M.Div.

Printed in the United States of America

ISBN 9781619965720

Cover Design by Natasha Cannon, Nspire Photography & Style
Nspire.ps@gmail.com

www.xulonpress.com

# Table of Contents

# Ackowledgements

Special thanks to my family and my church family at Progressive Baptist Church in Indianapolis for your love and support. Your patience and kindness toward me have helped me to make this project possible. I must confess that you all have also been instrumental in my desire to learn how to pray. Family, biological, extended and church, will force you to get on your knees.

I want to thank Stephanie Rice for her friendship and encouragement. She has offered me the benefit of learning from her experience. She self-published a wonderful book called "Welcome to the Valley" several years ago. It is a tremendous testimony about surviving and growing through a serious season of unemployment. As a result of her experience, I have saved much time and avoided many mistakes. The Steph-o-lotuion will not be televised . . . it is already LIVE!

I want to thank my Godchildren who are such an important part of my life. God did not bless me with biological children, but I have the most amazing Godchildren ever. Much of what I do is for them because they are the greatest inspiration in my life. I desire for all of them to have a powerful and personal relationship with God as they continue to grow up and grow in grace. I am extremely proud of them. Their names are Toi Denise, Onya, Chad, Natasha (aka Jolly Rancher) Tiffany, Ambria (aka Baby Girl), Corrin, Tavia (aka Princess), Meka, John Jr., Evan Michael, Cameron, and Dakarai.

I want to thank Leslie Carpenter, Marya Jones and Laquilla Hobson for their patience and constructive criticism as they assisted me in editing and proofreading this book. They all know that I am more of a talker than a writer. If there is any good quality to the writing, the credit goes to God and to them. If not, the blame all falls to me. All three of these ladies are very special to me and I know that they have my best interest at heart. It is good to KNOW that there are some people in your corner.

Special thanks to Karen Merriwether for being a constant source of support and encouragement. Whenever I was tempted to quit or just needed to vent, you were there. I couldn't have done it without you.

The cover of this book is absolutely beautiful and it was created by my lovely goddaughter, Natasha, and her new company Nspire Photography & Style. She is a super talented photographer and designer. Her work has made me look better than I could have with anyone else because this cover was created by love. Thanks J.R. (smile).

I must thank God for the inspiration and the anointing that I know are on these pages. God is up to something big and PRAYER is the key that we need to access what God is doing.

Finally, I want to thank you for taking the time to join me on this journey. Because we have had this interaction, I believe that we are knit together for such a time as this. As we build an army of prayer warriors, I believe that God is going to use us to get the church on one accord. When that happens, God's power will be released like we have not seen in generations. Get ready!

# Forward

## Dr. Stephen J. Clay

Pastor Michael K Jones' most recent book entitled **Lord Teach Me to Pray** is indeed essential for those seeking a deeper and abiding relationship with God. Pastor Jones' practical approach to daily prayer and spiritual development are presented in such a concise and helpful manner. It is akin to a journey. At the end you will discover that you are stronger and far more equipped to handle the challenges of life.

This book is designed to bring power into your prayer life. However, if you are content with a powerless prayer life then this book is not for you. This book is designed to teach you how to unleash the prayer warrior in you, so you can experience the sweet victory of answered prayer for you, your family, and the church.

Pastor Jones' analysis of the Lord's Prayer as a model to enhance our daily prayer life is refreshing, clear, and helpful. This book is one of the best tools for spiritual development that I have come across in a long time. Born out of Pastor Jones' own walk with God, he has managed to bring the wealth of his academic training and his personal experience into syntheses for the development of those in the body of Christ.

Pastor Jones makes it clear that prayers God answers are those which reflect God's will in the world. Often times many people turn prayer into a "wish list" or worse a "to do list" for God. This book seeks to guide you through how to develop a prayer life that honors God. If applied, it will release the power of God in your life to bring about the desired results.

The author begins with stressing the importance of developing a personal relationship with God. This is fundamental to having your prayers answered. Knowing God is better than just knowing about him. This book will create in you a thirst to know God better, talk to him more often, and to pray the types of prayers that can change your life. So, get ready to grow, as you grow share the journey with a friend and expose them to the power and practice of daily prayer.

As a result your life will be better and the body of Christ will be stronger!

# Part One

# The Introduction to Prayer

# Introduction

This book is intended to deepen your understanding of the power and practice of prayer. What you will find in this material is a Biblically based discussion on what prayer is, and why so many people are unable to pray effectively. You will also find a detailed study of The Lord's Prayer as an example of the component parts of effective prayer. Finally, several practical steps will be shared that will enhance your prayer life.

If you take the time to delve deeply into the heart of this material, I guarantee that it will have a dramatic and positive effect on your life. I am able to guarantee results because all of this material is based on the Bible, The Word of God. The Word of God is life and power and if applied properly, results must come. In fact, the Bible states that - all who ask, seek or knock will find answers, discover truth, and find open doors!

So if you have been a Christian for any length of time without answers, revealed truths or opened doors, it could be that you need to develop in the area of prayer.

The teaching of Jesus will bring clarity to our conversation. The Gospel according to Matthew gives us the most comprehensive record of a sermon that Jesus preached to the multitudes. It is called The Sermon on the Mount and is found in Matthew chapters five through seven. This very practical sermon expresses the essentials for living a successful Christian life. As a central theme of the sermon, Jesus teaches us how to pray. Join me in the scripture as Jesus sets some ground rules that we must be aware of if we are to be successful in prayer.

But thou, when thou prayest enter into thy closet, and when thou has shut the door, pray to the Father which is in secret: and thy Father which seeth in secret shall reward thee openly.

But when ye pray, use not vain repetitions, as the heathen do: for they think that they shall be heard for their much speaking.

Be not ye therefore like unto them: for your Father knoweth what things ye have need of, before ye ask him (Matt 6:6-9 KJV).

When we pray, God wants quiet, one-on-one, time with us. In Jesus' day, the Pharisees would pray loudly on the street corners just so people would notice them and see how self-righteous they were. These religious leaders prayed for show and the recognition of people. Prayer for them was not about spending quality time with God, but to impress their human audience.

God wants us to come to Him without pomp or circumstance, recognition or display. When we actually make time to pray, most of us do so without pomp or circumstance. Unfortunately, however, the reality is that far too many of us don't give a thought to prayer at all except to bless our food or to ask for safety through the night as we are falling asleep. We generally bless food out of routine and at bedtime we are so tired that when we pray we tend to trail off into dreamland somewhere in the middle of it.

Because of our casual and lackadaisical approach to prayer we often wonder why it seems God doesn't hear or answer our prayers. Perhaps our prayers get muffled somewhere in between the snoring and the TV left on for background noise. Maybe our prayers are out of alignment with scripture and the will of God. Or, since all things happen or don't within God's will, perhaps the answer is no and we just don't like to be told no!

The biggest reason most of us never get results with prayer is because we are not seeking the things of God. We tend to use prayer to either appear holy in our own eyes or in the estimation of others, or to make demands on God. As a serious pastor and teacher, I have discovered personally that God will not tolerate any of that manipulative and inappropriate behavior.

After establishing the ground rules, Jesus gave us a model for prayer:

"After this manner therefore pray ye:
Our Father which art in heaven, Hallowed be thy Name.
Thy kingdom come, Thy will be done in earth, as it is in heaven.
Give us this day our daily bread.

And forgive us our debts, as we forgive our debtors.

And lead us not into temptation but deliver us from evil:

For thine is the kingdom, and the power, and the glory, forever." (Matt. 6:9-13 KJV).

Just a few verses down Jesus instructs us:

"Lay not up for yourselves treasures upon earth, where moth and rust doth corrupt, and where thieves break through and steal:

But lay up for yourselves treasures in heaven, where neither moth nor rust doth corrupt, and where thieves do not break through nor steal:

For where your treasure is, there will your heart be also." (Verse 19-21 KJV).

Many pastors and churches teach that every little materialistic thing we want is just a prayer away. We have been guilty of teaching that prayer is a power or force directed at God to which He is then obligated to respond. We teach the name it and claim it, blab it and grab it, model of prayer.

That is not the way it works with God. In fact, just before Jesus gives us the model prayer, He reminds us that God knows what we need before we ask. God does not want us to spend our time with Him rambling on about the things we want or need. He doesn't desire our "wish lists," He wants our hearts. He wants us to get to know Him and to discover His great love for us. He wants our love and respect, not our demands. Who are we to demand anything of Him anyway? He is GOD, we are not.

Unfortunately, many of us make prayer our time of rattling off what we want or need and never move on to anything else. We claim we don't do that because, after all, we throw in a few other things to masque it, but we are only kidding ourselves and the Lord is not amused. He is patient, but not amused, when the main focus of prayer time is spent on what we want in regard to this world and the things in it.

If we really understood God's love for humanity we would be praying that the Holy Spirit would convict the wicked and lead us to repentance and salvation instead of praying for another car, house, winning lottery numbers or whatever else we think would make our lives easier. The Bible challenges us to be in the world but not of the world! Ring a bell?

Didn't the Master say "lay not up for yourselves treasures on this earth?" Yet most people pray and seek the things of this earth. We make worldly needs our number one priority while, the things He wants us to make our number one priority - laying up treasures in heaven - we tend to completely ignore.

I had to learn this myself years ago. I was always praying with no power and with little effect. All I had been taught was to use prayer to ask for things . . . and boy did I ask. Unfortunately, I was often disappointed with prayer when most of the things on my request list never materialized. I knew prayer was critical to living a successful Christian life yet I had no idea of how to pray and no understanding of the real purpose of prayer. So I asked God to teach me how to pray. God's answer to me is this book.

Turn the page, and get ready to begin a journey that will change your life. You are on your way to becoming a **prayer warrior.**

## Chapter 1

# Setting the Foundation

The 15th chapter of the Gospel of St. John is one of the most profound discussions of prayer found in the entire Bible. In this chapter, Jesus declares with great clarity and incredible detail the essence of prayer.

Before we go any further, if you do not have your Bible with you, stop and go get it. You will not get the full benefit of this experience without it.

Good! Now that you have your Bible, take 5 minutes and read the entire 15th chapter of the Gospel of John. Read up to and including the first verse of chapter 16, (It is OK if you read it more than once. Actually, that is preferable.) Pay particular attention to chapter 15 verse 7, but read the entire passage.

Excellent! Now we are ready to begin our journey into the study of prayer. Turn the page and let's get to work!

## What is prayer?

The very first thing that you should notice from reading this chapter is that it is fundamentally about relationships. Notice Jesus' words in verse 5:

"I am the vine, ye are the branches: He that abideth in me and I in him, the same bringeth forth much fruit: for without me ye can do nothing." (KJV)

These words describe an intense and extremely intimate relationship. The main point to be understood is that prayer is essentially about a relationship; your relationship with God. Now before you run past this statement too quickly, think about any substantive relationship that you have. They all require time, energy, effort and struggle in order for them to be successful. No relationship of any value happens without effort on the part of the people in the relationship.

This is what makes our focus on verse 7 so important. Verse 7 is a promise from Jesus. It reads as follows:

"If you abide in me, and my words abide in you, ye shall ask what you will, and it shall be done unto you." (KJV)

The key to power and success in prayer is understanding first and foremost that prayer is **not** about getting the things you want from God. **Rather, it is about getting to know God!** Take a minute to think about this. It is important for us to realize that prayer is about our **personal relationship** with God. As long as we think of prayer as a means to acquire things or to get circumstances and events to go our way, we will never be able to harness the true power of prayer.

Let me offer an example:

Have you ever pleaded with God in prayer asking Him to give you some "thing" or to change (fix) some person or situation and found that your prayer request was not answered?

Have you noticed in your own prayer life that in many instances it appears that God does not hear you?

Christians are quick to claim that prayer is powerful and that *"Prayer Changes Things,"* however, if we look at the Church, it does not seem that our claims about prayer agree with reality. If prayer worked like that, then all Christians would be rich in worldly possessions and would be in control of other people and circumstances. In fact, that kind of prayer would make us gods and cause God to be our servant.

On the other hand, if we were all praying in line with the word and will of God, then our Churches would be full of growing, dedicated, committed people, who were kind, forgiving, nonjudgmental, loving and faithful. We would also have such an impact on our society that our cities would not be the violent and perverted places that they are today.

This tells me that either . . .

1) Prayer does not work; or,

2) That Christians are not praying; or,

3) Christians do not know how or why we pray.

Since God has always proven faithful and His word is true, we know that the first proposition is false. Just remember John 15:7. If we abide in Him and His word abides in us then we can ask what we will and it shall be done! According to the Holy Scripture, the promise of prayer is secure.

I am convinced that the problem is not with the promise of prayer. Rather, it is that many Christians do not pray at all, and of the ones who do, **most** do not know how to pray! This is confirmed in the book of James.

James chapter 4: 2-3 states the following:

"Ye lust and have not: ye kill, and desire to have, and cannot obtain: ye fight and war, **yet ye have not, because ye ask not. Ye ask, and receive not, because ye ask amiss, that ye may consume it upon your lusts**." (Emphasis is mine) (KJV).

The Bible addresses the question that we are asking.

> *If Prayer is so powerful, then why are Christians living such powerless lives?*

James says that it is not a problem with the promise of prayer. It is a problem with those of us who are praying. Some, James states, do not ask at all. Others, James declares ask for the wrong reasons. They ask so that they can have something **only** for themselves; something to squander on their own lust.

I know this from personal experience. When I was first called to a ministry of prayer, I spent most my time seeking God's **HAND**. All I wanted was for God to do this or that. As I began to grow in prayer I was blessed to be instructed by a Deacon who had been committed to daily prayer for over thirty years. I learned that my prayers were often ineffective because I should have been seeking God's **FACE** not simply trying to get things from God's **HAND**. This means that I should have been longing for God's friendship and fellowship. I should have been asking God to help me to be the person He created me to be - one made in His image and designed to worship Him. I should have been asking for him to save me, deliver me, develop me and then use me as an instrument to help save, deliver and develop others.

Prior to my training in prayer, I wanted for God to give me what I wanted, when I wanted it, how I wanted it, because I wanted it. I was truly a babe in Christ when it came to prayer even though I was already serving as a minister and preaching the Gospel on a regular basis. I must have looked like a spoiled brat to God, but God was having none of it. Like a small child, I would make demands on God to do what I wanted and would have spiritual temper tantrums if things did not go my way. Fortunately, God would lovingly say "no" and help me to mature in my relationship with him. My Heavenly Father was always patient and loving with me as He taught me that giving me what I want on my terms was not what was best for me.

I am learning to trust my Heavenly Father to know and to do what is best for me. This is the path to spiritual maturity that we must all go through. God is a loving parent who will work with all of His children to lead us to maturity. In fact, scripture teaches us that God, who began the good work in us, will continue His work until it is finally finished. (See Philippians. 1:6) God lovingly and mercifully began to train me and lead me toward spiritual maturity through prayer.

Don't be discouraged if you are a "babe in Christ" in your prayer life. We all start in that position. The reality is that the minute you begin to talk to God, even in temper tantrums, is a sign that God has begun a work in you! Rest assured, if you don't quit on God, God will never quit on you! In fact, remember the promise of God from Philippians 1:6. If God has started raising you up towards maturity, He will not stop until you reach your destiny in Him.

## *Moving Beyond Temper Tantrums in Prayer*

In order to harness the power of prayer we must learn to abide in Him and to allow His word to abide in us. This means that we must learn to seek His face and not His hands. We must understand that Prayer is **not** an invitation to demand that God give us the things that we want. Instead prayer is an invitation to enter into the personal, holy, and heavenly relationship that we need. Only then will we begin to pray with power **and whatever we ask of God will be done.**

This is so because as we grow in our relationship with God and allow His word to grow in us, we cannot be selfish in prayer. We cannot simply ask for the things that we want. Instead, we will ask God to enhance our relationship with Him. As we grow in this personal relationship with God, we will discover that God desires to prosper and bless us with every good thing anyway. We don't have to beg God for divine favor and blessing, we just have to understand who we are to Him. Because we are His children and He is our Father, He wants us to be successful, happy, healthy and blessed.

> *The most important thing that you can do to access power in prayer is to work on your personal relationship with God through Jesus Christ.*

You must understand that God loves you! You must come to accept that God loves you so much that God sent His only begotten Son, Jesus, to die on Calvary's cross for your sins. You must believe that God raised Jesus from the dead to demonstrate His power over life and death. You must understand that God does not judge you on the basis of your morality or personal goodness. Instead, God judges you on the basis of your belief in and acceptance of Jesus' sacrifice on the cross for your sins. Your relationship with God is not based on how good you are. It is based on your believing God and accepting what God has done for you.

"For if you confess with your mouth that Jesus is Lord and believe in your heart that God raised him from the dead, you will be saved. For it is by believing in your heart that you are made right with God and it is by confessing with your mouth that you are saved. As the scriptures tell us, 'anyone who believed in him will not be disappointed." (Romans 10:9-11 NAS)

Your salvation and your personal relationship with God, made possible by the sacrifice of Jesus Christ, are vitally important. In case you are still uncertain, let me illustrate with the powerful story of Navy Seal Petty Officer 2nd Class Michael Monsoor. Please read the account as reported on Navyseal.com:

"On 29 September (2006), Monsoor was part of a sniper overwatch security position in eastern Ramadi, Iraq, with three other SEALs and eight Iraqi soldiers. They were providing overwatch security while joint and combined forces were conducting missions in the area. Ramadi had been a violent and intense area for a very strong and aggressive insurgency for some time. All morning long the overwatch position received harassment fire that had become a typical part of the day for the security team. Around midday, the exterior of the building was struck by a single rocket propelled grenade (RPG), but no injuries to any of the overwatch personnel were sustained. The overwatch couldn't tell where the RPG came from and didn't return fire."

"A couple of hours later, an insurgency fighter closed on the overwatch position and threw a fragment grenade into the overwatch position which hit Monsoor in the chest before falling in front of him. Monsoor yelled, "Grenade!" and dropped on top of the grenade prior to it exploding. Monsoor's body shielded the others from the brunt of the fragmentation blast and two other SEALs were only wounded by the remaining blast."

"One of the key aspects of this incident was the way the overwatch position was structured. There was only one access point for entry or exit and Monsoor was the only one who could have saved himself from harm. Instead, knowing what the outcome would be, he fell on the grenade to save the others from harm. Monsoor and the two injured were evacuated to the combat outpost battalion aid station where Monsoor died approximately 30 minutes after the incident from injuries sustained by the grenade blast."

Also due to Monsoor's selfless actions, the fourth man of the SEAL squad who was 10-15 feet from the blast was unhurt. A 28-year-old Lieutenant, who sustained shrapnel wounds to both legs that day, said the following in crediting Monsoor with saving his life: "He never took his eye off the grenade – his only movement was down toward it. He undoubtedly saved mine and the other Seal's lives, and we owe him."

As Kristen Scharnberg of the Chicago Tribune summarized in tribute, "The men who were there that day say they could see the options flicker across Michael Monsoor's face: save himself or save the men he had long considered brothers. He chose them."

The story of Michael Monsoor is a modern day representation of the work of Salvation that Jesus has provided for us. Due to our sin and the activities of our enemy – the devil – we are in battle and under attack. Often, we are not able to determine where the attack is coming from. Sometimes we seem to be taking fire from all sides; financial, emotional, relational, and personal. It can be so overwhelming that we don't know how to fight back.

Before long, just like the men in the above account, the enemy will get so close that he will try to take us out. The Bible puts it this way: the thief (the devil) comes to steal, kill and destroy. (See John 10:10). That is when the grenade lands in our situation. Here is where Michael Monsoor made the most remarkable choice. He could have saved himself and let all of the others with him die. He had a means of escape. Instead of saving himself, he sacrificed himself so that all of those with him could live.

When you come to know Jesus as your personal savior, you accept the fact that Jesus decided to fight your battles with you and for you so that you could win. Jesus then sacrifices Himself and takes the grenade that was meant for you. Jesus dies so that you can have an awesome life. In fact, the bible states that God so loved the world that He sent His son Jesus so that whoever believes in Him will live forever. (See John 3:16)

Michael Monsoor posthumously received the Medal of Honor from President George W. Bush. It was presented to Michael's father at the White House. The soldiers who were saved were all at the ceremony. Because of Michael Monsoor's sacrifice, each of the saved soldiers now wants to have a special relationship with his father. They all stated that while they could not replace his son, they would do their best to be sons to him. They also wanted him to be a father to them. They wanted to learn the lessons that Michael's father taught him that made him into the man who would sacrifice his life for them.

Do you see the picture? That is exactly what Jesus has done for you. He did not have to die. Jesus could have saved Himself and let you die. Instead, he chose you! He chose me! If you accept what Jesus has done for you, you will desire an intimate relationship with God and by faith you will become His child. You can become an adopted daughter or son of God right now. I invite you to pause now and accept Jesus as your savior (the one who died for you as a result of your sins). If you have already accepted Jesus by believing that he died for your sins and that God raised him from the dead, then pause and thank God for dying for you, saving you, loving you and accepting you as His child. If you are not in a personal relationship with God, please say the following prayer:

*Father in Heaven, I believe that you are God and that Jesus is Your Son. I believe that Jesus died for my sins and that after three days, He arose from the dead. Thank you for paying my debt and for saving my life. Because of what your Son Jesus did for me, I am saved. I will not die an eternal death but instead, I have been given eternal life. Today I also make an informed decision to turn from my past ways and to travel through life with you. Jesus, I ask You to come into my heart to be Lord and Savior of my life. Make something and someone new of me. Create in me a hunger for Your Word. By Your Spirit lead me to a church where I can gather together with other believers and be taught Your promises and principles accurately and without compromise. I want to fully understand my responsibility and authority as Your child. Thank You for salvation and for the promise of abundant and eternal life -- Spiritually, physically, economically and socially. Father, I am determined to give Your name the praise, honor, and glory with my words and with my life from now on. In the name of Jesus Christ I pray, AMEN.*

In the next chapter, we will address the questions:

How can I claim the promise of John 15:7?

What does it mean to abide in Him and to have His word abide in me?

How can I move from seeking God's hand to seeking God's face?

Before we move on to the next chapter, take the time to answer the following review questions. After writing answers to the review questions, move to the next chapter and expect a miracle.

**Review Questions:**

1) Prayer is not about getting things. Instead, prayer is primarily about a personal _____ with _____.

2) There is no problem with the promise of prayer. The problem is with us. James 4: 2-3 teaches us that we have not because we _____. He continues and says that ye ask and receive not _____

_____

_____.


3) Read Psalm 27 in its entirety. After reading this Psalm why do you think that it is critical that we learn to seek God's face more than seeking things from God's hand?

_____

_____

_____

_____

_____

_____

_____

Before you go on to the next chapter, take 5 minutes and thank God for being our Heavenly Father. Thank God that you can have a personal, intimate relationship with Him. Thank God that you can seek His face and ask God to open your heart and mind to His Word. Do this while meditating on John 15:7. You should know this verse by now. It says:

> *"If you abide in me, and my words abide in you, ye shall ask what you will, and it shall be done unto you." (KJV)*

**REMEMBER** that the power and the purpose of prayer are all about having a personal relationship with GOD!

## Chapter 2

# Take Time to Be Holy

There is a wonderful hymn entitled *Take Time to Be Holy*. The words of this song express the essence of abiding in Him and allowing His word to abide in us. Remember from the previous chapter that the key to harnessing the power of prayer is based on our choice to abide in Him and allowing His word to abide in us; it is based on our developing a personal and mature relationship with God through Jesus Christ.

John 15:7 is an "if . . . then" phrase. If we do something, then God will do for us whatever we ask of Him. So what does it mean to abide? Read the words to this hymn and then we will talk about it.

Take time to be holy, speak oft with thy Lord;

Abide in Him always, and feed on His Word.

Make friends of God's children, help those who are weak,

Forgetting in nothing His blessing to seek.


Take time to be holy, the world rushes on;

Spend much time in secret, with Jesus alone.

By looking to Jesus, like Him thou shalt be;

Thy friends in thy conduct His likeness shall see.


Take time to be holy, let Him be thy guide,

And run not before Him, whatever be tide.

In joy or in sorrow, still follow the Lord,

And, looking to Jesus, still trust in His Word.


Take time to be holy, be calm in thy soul,

Each thought and each motive beneath His control.

Thus led by His Spirit to fountains of love,

Thou soon shalt be fitted for service above.


This is quite a song. It really says it all. But let's take a few minutes to discuss the meaning and power of this great hymn. If you are continuing from the last chapter without a break then you still have your Bible with you. If you are returning to our conversation after a break, don't forget your Bible. You will need it. In this chapter we will discover how to abide in Him.

The answer in its simplest terms is that **if we are to abide in Him, we must take time to be holy.**

Turn your Bible to Psalm 15. In the first verse, David asks the very same question that we are asking. He asks: "Lord, who shall abide in thy tabernacle? Who shall dwell in thy holy hill?"

The remainder of this Psalm is the answer to that question. Read the rest of the psalm and take a few minutes to allow the words to speak to you.

Good, I hope that you read it slowly and more than once. Take time to let the words speak to you. There is no rush; you can read the Psalm again before we continue.

Are you ready now? Good. Turn the page and let's continue.

Psalm 15 is critically important to accessing the power of prayer. This is so because it offers us the key to unlock the promise of John 15:7. This Psalm teaches us what it means to abide in Him. Immediately you should have discovered that abiding is more than saying our prayers once in a while and it means more than coming to church once a week.

This Psalm says that what is most important in our prayer life is not what words we say. What is most important is the lifestyle that we live. David is saying that if we want our prayer life to be powerful; if we want our prayers to have influence in heaven; if we want to abide on God's holy hill; then we must have a vital and vibrant relationship with God.

This means that our life and lifestyle must reflect the reality of our relationship with God. This requires that we slow down long enough to take time to be holy.

> *Prayer is not so much what we say, prayer is how we live! Prayer is a lifestyle – one determined and defined by our relationship with God.*

It is critical to understand that being holy; living a moral lifestyle, is not by itself proof of a personal relationship with God. Belief in the finished work of Jesus Christ on the Cross is what establishes our relationship with God. God is not asking us to be holy and then He will be in a relationship with us. God is asking us to be in a relationship with Him, and then he will empower us to be holy.

God is not looking for perfect people to be in relationship with Him. God is looking for people who accept the sacrifice of Jesus Christ for the forgiveness of their sins. Believing in Jesus is what makes us righteous in the eyes of God.

That, however, is not the end of the story. As a result of this belief, God desires to go to work on us to perfect us and transform us into the likeness of His first born Son, Jesus. God literally wants to change us. If we let God have His way, our thinking changes, our vocabulary changes, our habits change, our actions change. In fact, we actually become new. The bible puts it this way: "Therefore, if any man [woman] be in Christ, he [she] is a new creature: old things are passed away, behold, all things are become new." (See 2 Corinthians 5-17 KJV)

The New Living Translation of the Bible states the same verse as follows: "What this means is that those who become Christians become new persons. They are not the same anymore, for the old life is gone. A new life has begun."

> *Literally, this means that if we are willing, God will begin to live in and through us! This is what makes us holy or righteous.*

So, what are the signs that God is at work in us to perfect us and make us new creatures? What signs should we look for to determine if we are able to abide in Him and have His word abide in us? Let's examine some keys from psalm 15.

> **Watch your mouth!**

In order to abide in God, we must watch what we say (see Psalm 15:2-3). We must bring our tongues under control and allow God to rule our mouths. In the New Living Translation of the Bible, the end of verse 2 states that we must speak the truth from a sincere heart. This verse does not mean that we are free to say whatever we think is true as long as we are sincere. It does not mean that we should declare that the hat the "old church lady" is wearing on Sunday is ugly because to us that is true and we are sincere.

The truth that this scripture is referring to is the truth of God as stated in the Bible. We must learn to speak what God has already said. Now I am not saying that we have to become a "super saint" who walks around quoting the bible all the time. What I am saying is that our conversation should line up with the spirit and principles of the word of God. Listen to what the bible says:

**"A man hath joy by the answer of his mouth: and a word spoken in due season, how good is it!" (Proverbs 15:23 KJV).**

According to this verse, there is joy in your mouth. If your words are not producing joy, then you are not in line with the word or will of God. I am not saying that you will never have dark days and tough times. I am saying that if you speak the word of God, you will discover that you can have joy no matter how dark or bright the day or how tough or easy the times. Joy is literally as close as the words in your mouth.

One of the greatest tragedies of Christianity is joyless Christians. One of the easiest tricks of our adversary, the devil, is to convince us to talk ourselves out of joy and into depression. Don't fall for it! Speak love! Speak life! Speak joy.

**"The thoughts of the wicked are an abomination to the LORD: but the words of the pure are pleasant words." (Proverbs 15:26 KJV)**

Pleasant, positive, affirming, life giving words should be in your mouth. You should be an encourager not a discourager; you should be optimistic, not pessimistic; you should speak life and not death. If you have a personal relationship with God through the sacrifice of Jesus Christ, you know that you have the victory because you know how the story ends! You know that God has a good plan for you and your life. Since you know the outcome, you should always speak in a positive manner. God's word declares that we know that God causes everything to work together for the good of those who love God and are called according to His purpose for them. (See Romans 8:28)

In fact, Proverbs 18:21 states: **"Death and life are in the power of the tongue."**

As you can clearly see, your words have tremendous power. If you want to be effective in prayer you should be careful about what comes out of your mouth. You cannot pray a life affirming prayer to God and then not speak life to yourself. You cannot ask God to heal you and then declare that you will never get well. You cannot ask for God to bless you and at the same time declare that you are cursed. You cannot say "I will never get any better." "This is just the way things are for me." "I guess I will never be happy." "I will never get out of this debt." "I will never get over this hurt."

Dear friend, you will never have power in prayer or in life if those are the words that come out of your mouth. First, they contradict the word and will of God. Second, you are what the bible calls double minded. The bible states that a double minded person should not expect to receive anything from the Lord. (James 1:6-8) Instead, you must speak in faith, believing what the word of God teaches. Your conversation must agree with God's word. If your confession matches God's word, you will have power with God and power in prayer.

Psalm 15:3 continues by stating that those who refuse to slander others, harm their neighbor, or speak evil of their friends, are the people who abide in God. (NLT). In essence, this verse states that we must also be careful what we say to and about others. Slander is when we speak negative things about others when we really don't know the truth. Another translation uses the word backbiting instead of slander. We must not say negative things behind other's backs. In fact, we must be careful not to speak negative things about others even if we have the facts and know the truth. If what we say will harm our neighbor or bring evil on our friends, we will not be effective in prayer. I am not telling you to keep silent when there is a crime or to avoid facing reality. I am telling you that if you are just speaking negative stuff, even if it is true, for the purpose of hurting others or bringing evil on friends, you will have trouble with God. If you are speaking negative things to get revenge or to somehow boost your self-esteem, self-image or prestige with others, you will have trouble with God. In fact, it is better to just not say anything negative about anyone if possible.

It is as simple as the wisdom that you probably learned from your mother or grandmother: "If you don't have anything good to say, don't say anything at all."

I want to challenge you to be positive in your speech. Begin to practice confessing what God says about you! Begin to speak life and not death into your life, your spouse's life, your children's' lives, your company's life, your church and even your enemies' lives and I can guarantee you that you will see great things happen. God is committed to His word. In fact, God says this about his words: "It is the same with my word. I will send it out, and it always produces fruit. It will accomplish all I want it to, and it will prosper everywhere I send it." (Isa 55:11 NLT). God is sending His word out through your mouth. Speak life and begin to live abundantly right now!

## *Do the right thing!*

In order to abide in God, we must also watch what we do! Psalm 15:2 says that we must walk uprightly and work righteousness. We must always try to do the right thing. The New Living Translations of this verse states that the ones who abide are those who lead blameless lives and do what is right. In other words, those who do the best that they can to treat themselves and others with grace, mercy and integrity are able to abide in Him. This means that we excuse others who make mistakes, we forgive those who wrong us, and we do our best not to offend or hurt others. It also means that we forgive ourselves for our mistakes and we ask for forgiveness from those who we have wronged.

This point seems to require a measure of spiritual maturity for us because we are tempted to operate like the world in which we live. Jesus worked hard to teach this lesson to his disciples in Bible days, and He continues to struggle with his modern day disciples too. Listen to the teaching of Jesus:

"But if you are willing to listen, I say, Love your enemies. Do good to those who hate you. Pray for the happiness of those who curse you. Pray for those who hurt you. If someone slaps you on one cheek, turn the other cheek. If someone demands your coat, offer your shirt also. Give what you have to anyone who asks you for it and when things are taken away from you, don't try to get them back. Do for others as you would like them to do for you.

Do you think you deserve credit merely for loving those who love you? Even the sinners do that. And if you do good only to those who do good to you, is that so wonderful? Even sinners do that much! And if you lend money only to those who can repay you, what good is that? Even sinners will lend to their own kind for a full return. Love your enemies! Do good to them! Lend to them! And don't be concerned that they might not repay. Then your reward from heaven will be very great, and you will truly be acting as children of the Most High, for he is kind to the unthankful and to those who are wicked. You must be compassionate, just as your Father is compassionate.

Stop judging others, and you will not be judged. Stop criticizing others, or it will all come back on you. If you forgive others, you will be forgiven. If you give, you will receive. Your gift will return to you in full measure, pressed down, shaken together to make room for more, and running over. Whatever measure you use in giving, large or small, it will be used to measure what is given back to you." (Luke 6:27-38) New Living Translation.

This teaching from Jesus is so powerful that I just had to quote the entire passage. This is not simply about treating people well who treat us well. The mandate is to treat the people who hate and hurt us in a loving and compassionate way. God promises that if we do that, He will repay us in such an overwhelming way that the blessings we receive will be very great and running over. God says that He will watch how we treat others and regardless of how they treat us, He will take care of us if we trust in Him.

When we enter into a personal relationship with God through the sacrifice of Jesus Christ, we must allow Jesus to show us how to be in that relationship. Jesus stated in the teaching quoted above that when we are compassionate and kind to the unthankful and wicked, we are acting like a child of the Most High. Jesus is literally painting a word picture of how our lives will change as we grow closer to God in this personal and abiding relationship.

Now, God knows that we will not be perfect! He knows that we are all growing in grace. This is an area where we must be diligent and determined to do our very best. I know personally how hard it is to bless those who are cursing you. I know how hard it is to love those who hate you. I also know that God never calls us to do what He will not empower us to do. If God says to do it, then we CAN do it. Jesus death and resurrection is our guarantee. If God's power can overcome death, surely, it is enough to empower us in life.

> *Never sell out your integrity!*

In order to abide, we must not take advantage of others for any reason. Psalm 15:4 teaches us that no opportunity or enticement should be able to move us from doing the right thing. This verse speaks to the reality that integrity is vital if we want to abide in Him and have his word abide in us. The New Living Translations records the verse as follows: [The people who abide in Him are] those who despise persistent sinners and honor the faithful followers of the Lord and keep their promises even when it hurts. (Psalm 15:4)

It appears that this verse is telling us that we should despise people who sin persistently. Literally, the verse is declaring that we should not honor those who choose to be wicked. We must treat the wicked with compassion but we must despise and even hate their behavior. This verse is one of the inspirations behind an old church phrase that admonishes us to hate the sin but love the sinner. We must be careful to never make excuses for sin and we must agree with God that all sin, especially our own persistent sin, is against God. It is important to understand that we are not called to hate ourselves either, but we must hate our sins.

Whenever God reveals to us our persistent sins, we must be quick to repent and ask God to help us to turn from our behavior. We are not called to beat ourselves up or to put ourselves down. Instead, we are called to come into agreement with God and to turn from our sins and turn toward God. When we discover persistent sins in others, while we hate their sin, we are called to love them. Remember what Jesus is trying to teach us: We are to have compassion on and forgiveness for those who are wicked – persistent sinners. We are to pray for them. We are not supposed to judge them. We are called to love them and then to place them and their sins into the hands of our Heavenly Father.

Finally, this verse states that we should keep our promises even when it hurts. That, my beloved, is a wonderful description of integrity. Many of us are always looking for the best deal. Now don't get me wrong, I believe in getting a good deal as much as the next person. The problem, however, is when we have made a commitment to a specific deal and then want to change because after the fact, "something better" comes along.

Permit me to share a personal example. As a pastor and preacher, I am often invited to preach the gospel in other locations and at other churches. There is a large church in a major city that I had dreamed of preaching in one day. The pastor of that church is internationally known and the opportunity would have elevated me in the eyes of my peers. Well, I was invited to speak in a small "store front" church which only had about 15 active church members. I was asked to come and preach for three nights in their revival service. I graciously accepted the invitation. About two weeks after I accepted the invitation at the very small church, I received a call from the mega-ministry and was invited to come and preach on the same nights.

I must be honest with you, I was so tempted to call the small church and cancel. After all, it was a dream come true to be able to stand and share the gospel in the mega-church. My peers would have been proud of me and I would have received a large honorarium. This was my great opportunity, but I had already made a commitment to the small church for those nights. Because of my understanding of the Word of God, I had to decline the mega-church request and fulfill my commitment at the small church.

Many of my peers laughed at my decision and challenged me to cancel on the small church. Instead, I kept my word and my commitment and preached in the small church. God showed up in those little services and many people were blessed. My peers laughed at my decision, but heaven rejoiced over it because I demonstrated integrity even when it hurt me financially and professionally. But guess what? God honored my decision to be faithful and blessed me with an opportunity two years later to preach at the mega-church on a Sunday morning. I preached all of the services and was blessed highly by God. Many people gave their lives to Jesus Christ and the pastor told me that he was led to give me the largest honorarium that he had ever given to a Sunday guest preacher.

God has a way of blessing us and seeing to it that we get WHAT we need WHEN we need it. It is critical to keep your word.

In summary, these three behaviors create a lifestyle that blesses God and causes us to abide in Him. Some of you reading this are saying, "Pastor Jones, I hear what you are saying but I just can't watch my mouth." "It is just too hard for me." Someone else is saying, "come on Pastor Jones, you really want me to bless MY enemies?" "Do you know what they have done to me?" "You can't possibly expect me to forgive them, so how in the world do you want me to bless them?" And some others are stating that there is no way that you will keep your word if it will hurt you. You figure that as long as you are honest with the people that you break your commitment to, that should be good enough. You rationalize, "they will understand." "They would do the same thing that I am doing if given half a chance."

Well, my sister or brother, we must make a commitment to God in and through Jesus Christ. I know that it seems impossible, but I want to show you some practical steps that you can take to move in the direction that God is calling you to move in. You can abide!

## The Promise of stability!

The last line in Psalm 15 in the New Living Translation states that the person who does the things mentioned above will stand firm forever. The New American Standard translation says: The person who does these things shall **never** be moved! In essence, the promise is that if we practice these things we will have stability in life. There is so much volatility in our world. The economy is tenuous. People are often fickle, fake and phony. Friends can be of the "fair-weather" variety and even family can be treacherous. Life is often very challenging and does not guarantee stability. The word of God however, promises that God will provide stability to those who trust Him and obey His word. This type of stability, real stability, cannot be bought. This can only come from God.

Imagine with me that your relationships could be stable; your job could be stable; your family could have stability. Imagine what your life would be like if your joy was stable; if your sense of peace was stable; if you truly had emotional stability . . . can you imagine it? Well, as you build your relationship with God by taking time to be holy, God promises that this can be your reality. You don't have to imagine it . . . you can live it!

Read the words of the song again. I will make it easy and print them again here:

Take time to be holy, speak oft with thy Lord;

Abide in Him always, and feed on His Word.

Make friends of God's children, help those who are weak,

Forgetting in nothing His blessing to seek.


Take time to be holy, the world rushes on;

Spend much time in secret, with Jesus alone.

By looking to Jesus, like Him thou shalt be;

Thy friends in thy conduct His likeness shall see.


Take time to be holy, let Him be thy guide,

And run not before Him, whatever be tide.

In joy or in sorrow, still follow the Lord,

And, looking to Jesus, still trust in His Word.


Take time to be holy, be calm in thy soul,

Each thought and each motive beneath His control.

Thus led by His Spirit to fountains of love,

Thou soon shalt be fitted for service above

This song provides a practical road map to an abiding relationship with God. This great hymn offers what I believe are practical steps that you and I can take to ensure that we are growing in the things that God wants us to do to abide in Him.

The first thing we should see from the song is that we must speak often with the Lord. This is done both literally through speaking to God in prayer and by feeding on God's Word. If you are not involved in a good Bible study; if you are not taking time out of your busy schedule to read and study the Word then you cannot abide. It is vitally important that you learn the Word of God. You must become a student of the Word. I am not saying that you have to be a bible scholar or go to Bible College. What I am saying is that you should be praying and asking God to give you a hunger for and an understanding of His word. You must make talking with God and learning from God's word a priority.

Reading books, like this one, which will teach you to pray, are crucial to your development as a Christian. You and I have entered in to a discipling relationship as you work through this material. God is using me to teach you to pray and encourage you to study God's Word. You will then use this book and other tools to enter into a discipling relationship with others. Together, God is using us to change a generation. As you internalize the truths in this book and get the Word of God deep down in your spirit, your life will never be the same. You will become rock solid as God blesses you with stability in every area of your life. Others will come to you to find out how they can be stable in such an unstable world. Your answer will be simple and profound - **because of your personal relationship with God through the person and work of Jesus Christ.**

Secondly, this work of learning the word and will of God must not merely be done at home. We must also do this at the church. The song rightly says make friends with God's children. This is done primarily through your active involvement in the local church. If you try to grow as a Christian at home alone, I can guarantee that you will fail in your effort. Because God designed us to be relational creatures, we need each other. You need to be a part of a local church. This is the place that God prepared to develop believers into full grown Christians. It is in the church that you will be taught bible principles. It is in the church that you will learn to put your faith into practice. It is in the church where you will hear a word of grace and forgiveness when you fall short. It is in church were you will sing the songs of Zion in a strange land. God designed the church to be a hospital for sinners and a place of restoration and blessing for all people.

That is why church membership is so important and why you should not jump from church to church whenever things don't seem to go your way. You must make a commitment to a local ministry, give yourself over to serve others and be a blessing to the ministry. You must become a tither of your time, your talent, and your money. You must find a place to get involved in ministry and if there is no ministry suited to your gifts, you should seek out your church leadership and request that the church create it. It is only through service that we grow and mature as Christians. If you are not active in your local church as a regular attendee in worship, a participant in Sunday school and bible study, and as a servant in some ministry, you will not be able to do what it takes to abide in Him.

Finally, this great hymn teaches us that we must yield control of our lives, our motives, our time, and our very selves to the Lord Jesus Christ. Whenever we find ourselves being self-centered, we must ask God to replace that attitude with one which is Christ-centered. Beloved, if you want to experience a new level of God's grace and joy, if you really want to enjoy the blessings and favor of God in your life then you are going to have to get your mind off of you and your selfish desires. You must learn to be a giver, not a taker. Please quit trying to figure out what everybody can do for you and start trying to figure out what you can do for someone else.

Isaiah 58:7- 9 says: "I want you to share your food with the hungry and to welcome poor wanders into your homes. Give clothes to those who need them and do not hide from relatives who need your help. If you do these things, your salvation [deliverance] will come like the dawn. Yes, your healing will come quickly. Your godliness will lead you forward, and the glory of the Lord will protect you from behind. Then you will call, the LORD will answer, 'Yes, I am here,' He will quickly reply." (New Living Translation).

When we make the time to do these things, we will begin to abide and as we begin to abide, we are on our way to accessing the power of prayer. God wants to answer your prayer. Most of all, God wants to be your friend and your Heavenly Father. God wants to have a personal relationship with you. Jesus has made that possible. If you want it, you can have it today! The favor of God is waiting for you!

In summary, we must take the time to think before we speak and to think before we act. What must we think about? We must always think about the Word of God before we speak or act. Paul puts it this way:

"Finally, brothers and sisters, whatsoever things are true, whatsoever things are honest, whatsoever things are just, whatsoever things are pure, whatsoever things are lovely, whatsoever things are of good report; if there be any virtue, and if there be any praise, think on these things." (Philippians 4:8 The New King James Version)

This means that we must meditate on the Word of God. Nothing else meets the above criteria. The Word must guide and direct us. In order to do that, we must take the time to study the Word so that we know the Word. Then we must be doers of the Word and not hearers only!

Before we move on to the next chapter, take the time to answer the following review questions. In the next chapter, we will begin a verse-by-verse analysis of the model prayer left to us by our Lord Jesus Christ. Now that we have established some basics about prayer and how it works, we will turn our attention to one of the most important questions that a Christian can ask: How do I pray?

**Review Questions:**

1) Why is it important for us to abide in Him and have his word abide in us? (See John 15:7 for the answer)

_____

_____

_____

2) As we consider what it means to abide in Him and let his word abide in us we stated that what is required is that we take time to be holy. In essence, what that means is that prayer is not so much what we say, rather prayer is how we

_____.

3) In order to abide in God we must do three things. We must watch what our _____. We must do the _____. We must not take advantage of others for any reason. No opportunity or enticement should be able to move us from doing the _____.

4) When we begin to live according to these principles Psalm 15 verse 5 promises that the person who does these things has the promise of _____.

5) Look at the words to the hymn *Take Time to be Holy*. List at least five things (three were written about in detail. You pick at least two other possibilities) that you should improve on so that you will grow in your relationship with God through Christ.

1. _____     2. _____
3. _____     4. _____
5. _____

Before you go on to the next chapter, take 5 minutes and ask God to help you commit to making the five things listed in the last question a vital part of your life, declare before God that you want to do His will and that you intend to establish your abode in Him and His Word. Commit to think before you speak or act. Determine that with the help of God you will **take time to be holy!**

# Part Two

# The Call To Prayer

# Introduction

According to the Biblical witness, people in days past literally heard God's voice. It essential that we hear His voice today as well. Hebrews 3:7-8 states: "wherefore as the Holy Ghost saith, **today** if ye will hear his voice, harden not your hearts as in the day of provocation, in the day of temptation in the wilderness." (KJV)

I believe that the Holy Spirit is speaking a word to the Church today. God is calling His Church to pray, and if we want to make a difference in this world, we need to listen. If we intend to be successful, powerful, and effective in these last days then we better learn that the victory comes: "Not by might, nor by power, but by my spirit saith the Lord." (Zechariah 4:6 KJV). I am convinced that God is calling His church to pray now more than ever before.

It is important for us to understand that the desire to pray is not something that we can work up in our own strength. The desire to pray is created in us by the Holy Spirit. Prayer is something that God initiates. If we could only grasp this simple truth we would be well on our way to transformation. The trouble is that this something that God does that is essentially a mystery: there are no neat formulas; no amount of books on prayer can ever reveal just what it is that God does.

Please remember that prayer is a relationship in which God is the initiator. God is constantly seeking to draw out a response from us. It is an ongoing relationship, and like any other relationship it cannot be programmed, labeled or packaged. It must be lived. It must be experienced. Therefore, prayer is a living, growing, and developing experience in and with God. This prayer lifestyle is not self-generated. It only occurs as we respond to God's incredible love for us and come to know Him as a result of Jesus' sacrifice on the cross for our sins. If you have accepted Jesus as your personal savior but have no desire to live for God and allow Him to live through you, don't worry. It may simply mean that you have not accepted Jesus as Lord just yet.

Before I confuse you, let me explain what the word "Lord" means in the context of Jesus Christ. Lord in the New Testament most often comes from the Greek word, kurios. It means supreme in authority. Here is a good example: When Saul (later to be known as Paul the Apostle) was traveling towards Damascus, something amazing happened. The story is recorded in Acts chapter 9:1-6 in the King James Version as follows:

[1]And Saul, yet breathing out threatenings and slaughter against the disciples of the **Lord**, went unto the high priest, [2]And desired of him letters to Damascus to the synagogues, that if he found any of this way, whether they were men or women, he might bring them bound unto Jerusalem. [3]And as he journeyed, he came near Damascus: and suddenly there shined round about him a light from heaven: [4]And he fell to the earth, and heard a voice saying unto him, Saul, Saul, why persecutest thou me? [5]And he said, Who art thou, **Lord**? And the **Lord** said, I am Jesus whom thou persecutest: it is hard for thee to kick against the pricks. [6]And he trembling and astonished said, **Lord**, what wilt thou

have me to do? And the **Lord** said unto him, Arise, and go into the city, and it shall be told thee what thou must do. (Acts 9:1-6 The King James Version – emphasis mine).

Where you see the word Lord in the passage above, you are reading the Greek word kurios meaning supreme in authority. Saul recognized the One speaking to Him as the Supreme Being of the universe. Saul asks the identity of the Lord, the One who is Supreme in Authority and the answer came back . . . Jesus!!!

Most of us pastors and teachers declare that one must accept Jesus as "Lord and Savior" to be saved. This phrase is not wrong but it can be very confusing. The problem is that some people have a different meaning for the word "Lord." If by using Lord, you mean that a person needs to trust Jesus Christ as the unique Son of God – Kurios or supreme authority - to be saved, the Bible agrees. If, by using Lord, you mean that a person must be willing to commit their life to serving God and complete obedience to God's will, the Scriptures do **NOT** agree that this is required for salvation. This second understanding of Lord is required for personal lifestyle change but not for salvation.

There is a life-long, growing in grace period for all who are saved but that grace period is not a condition of their salvation. No Christian can ever claim to have arrived at sinless perfection in this life. We are all sinners saved by God's grace. It does not matter how good a Christian you may think you are, the fact is, you and I are nobodies without God. The Apostle Paul explained this truth as follows in Galatians 6:3, "For if a man think himself to be something, when **HE IS NOTHING**, he deceiveth himself." (Emphasis mine).

In order to be saved, you only need to trust in the Lord for his finished work on the cross. You do NOT need to do anything to be saved except admit you're a sinner and then accept the sacrifice of Jesus on the cross as full payment for your sins. You do NOT have to give up your sins to be saved either . . . except one—the sin of unbelief! You do not have to dedicate your life to serving Him or obeying all of his commands. This may happen immediately or come later but it has nothing to do with being saved.

When a lost sinner turns to Christ for salvation, they have turned from their old way of thinking to a new belief system that is built on the sacrifice of Jesus on the Cross. This is Biblical repentance; a turning point; a change of mind; a foundational change in belief system. If you are truly repentant then you will struggle concerning your sins because you won't have the arrogant attitude that you can happily continue living in sin. If you are sincere, then you will continue to feel convicted over you sins and failures throughout your life. **Here is the good news:** God does not expect you to clean up your act in order to be saved. On the contrary, He wants to help you clean up your act **after** you've been saved. Just as lost people cannot save themselves; neither can believers live the Christian life apart from the Holy Spirit of God. We absolutely need God to help us along the way. **We are saved by grace through faith and not of works so that we can't take any credit. Once saved, we are only able to live the Christian life by making a choice to let Jesus Christ take control of our lives and change us from the inside out.**

Jesus said, "For God so loved the world, that he gave his only begotten Son, that whosoever believeth in him should not perish, but have everlasting life" (John 3:16). That settles it for salvation.

So, what most pastors and teachers mean when they say that you should "make Jesus the Lord of your life" is that you begin the process of giving Jesus complete control of your life. Though this is a wonderful change in the life of any believer, it is NOT a requirement for salvation. Again, the Bible speaks of growing in grace: "But **GROW IN GRACE**, and in the knowledge of our Lord and Savior Jesus Christ. To him be glory both now and forever. Amen." (2nd Peter 3:18 - King James Version). Every Christian needs to grow in grace but it is impossible for a new believer in Christ to have the understanding and discernment that a mature Christian would have. It is an ongoing process. "As newborn babes, desire the sincere milk of the word, that ye may **GROW** thereby" (1st Peter 2:2 – King James Version). The Christian life is all about changing over time and becoming more like Jesus in our daily lives. If we are to succeed in this process then moment by moment, we must ask the Holy Spirit to show us areas in our life that need improvement and allow His will to be formed in us. This is the benefit **of** salvation but not a requirement **for** salvation.

So, if you do not have the desire to pray or to change and are not having much success living the Christian life, you can change that right now by making Jesus the Lord of your life. Just pray this simple prayer:

*Lord, Jesus! Thank you for your finished work on Calvary's cross. Thank you for dying in my place and paying the price for all of my sins – past, present and future. I receive my salvation with great joy. Now Lord Jesus, I make a choice to change. I don't want to continue to live like I have been living. I know that You can and will make me better. Right now, I give you access to every area of my life and I ask you to send your Holy Spirit to point out where I am wrong and to give me the power to change and live right. AMEN!*

If, however, God has already created a **desire** to pray in your heart and you are doing your best, then I hope that you will go deeper into prayer as you continue to grow in grace through this teaching.

Whatever your situation, ask God to give you a heart to pray. Then pray that God will help you transform that **desire** into a **daily discipline**. As the discipline to pray is formed within you, soon you will find that **discipline** will be transformed into a sheer **delight.**

Let me offer an example.

How often do you sit down and decide that you are going to spend some time in prayer with God? For some people, an honest answer is rarely, if at all. For others it may be often. For those who attempt to spend time in prayer, how often do you find that about 2 minutes into your prayer time, your mind begins to wander and before you know it you are either asleep or thinking about anything and everything but spending time with your Heavenly Father?

If you can identify with this experience, don't feel bad. This is a common occurrence for most of us. When Jesus was in the garden of Gethsemane he asked his disciples "Could you not watch with me one hour? Watch and pray, that ye enter not into temptation: the spirit is indeed willing but the flesh is weak" (Matt 26:40-41 KJV). The same Jesus is asking us to join Him in prayer and to take our time! Many of us are just like the disciples; our spirits are willing but the flesh is weak!

This is why I say that prayer is something that God does. He implants in us the desire to pray. As we begin to act on that divinely inspired desire, prayer becomes less difficult and is transformed into a delight by His grace. Just like any relationship is often awkward in the beginning and becomes more enjoyable as we get to know one another, so too with God and our time in prayer. As we continue to be consistent in prayer, it moves beyond an obligation and discipline to complete delight. This section of the book is designed to help us find the discipline to pray with more focus and to spend all of the time needed to build our relationship with God. If you internalize this material it will give you a path - if you stick to it - which will move you from failure to freedom and from discipline to delight in prayer.

> *Remember, John 15:7: If we abide . . .*
> *then God will answer.*

God desires to see your heart transformed into a house of prayer. Why? Because there is so much that God wants to do for you and through you. Again, please don't miss what I just shared. God wants to bless you! That is certain. But God also want to use you to be a blessing to others. In fact, that is one of the main reasons why God blesses you. I believe that there are only two reasons why God blesses any of us. First, and most importantly, is because God loves us! Secondly is because God wants to show His love to others by using us to be a blessing to them.

Therefore, as you begin to get disciplined in prayer, a very simple yet profound progression will take place within you. Allow me a few more moments to explain what I mean.

It was a normal routine day in the temple at Jerusalem until the moment Jesus walked in. What He saw made Him both heartbroken and angry. After making a whip from some cords, Jesus made His way toward the money changers and the people buying and selling animals for sacrifices and forcefully drove them, their animals, and their money out of the temple. Before the amazed congregation could react, Jesus was back, this time to knock over the tables and seats of the money changers and animal traders. The scattered coins were probably still whirling and rolling across the floor when Jesus yelled with righteous indignation: "My house shall be called the house of prayer, but ye have made it a den of thieves." (Matt 21:13 KJV)

Recognizing that only the guilty had anything to fear, the blind and lame ran to Jesus in the temple and He healed them. In the background everyone could hear the voices and laughter of happy children singing and shouting Hosanna.

(Hosanna means praise the Lord). When the Chief Priest and scribes angrily demanded that Jesus quiet the children's praise to God, He calmly responded, "Yea; have ye never read, Out of the mouth of babes and sucklings thou hast perfected praise?" (This Bible story is found in Matt 21:12-16 KJV).

Take a moment to study the amazing sequence of events in these verses. First, Jesus cleansed the temple causing it to become a house of **purity** by throwing out those who had made the temple in to a den of thieves. (Verse 12). Then Jesus made the pronouncement: it would be called a house of **prayer.** (Verse 13). Next the temple was transformed into a house of **power** as the blind and the lame came to Jesus and he healed them there. (Verse 14). And finally, the temple became a house of **praise.** (Verse 16).

What I want you to understand is that the same sequence of events can and will take place in the Church and in you if you get serious about prayer. Paul says "Know ye not that ye are the temple of God, and that the Spirit of God dwelleth in you?" (1 Cor. 3:16 KJV). You are part of the church that God wants to live in by filling you with His Holy Spirit (Eph. 2:20-22). But all too often our temples are polluted by greed, misguided motives and selfish sin.

It is a travesty for believers to talk one way and live another. God will not continue to bless an impure church and God will not sanction and pour out overwhelming favor on impure Christians. Remember, you must learn to abide in Him and have His word abide in you if you intend to ask what you will and have it done. God's church will not become the house of power and perfected praise until it allows the Holy Spirit to purify its self-righteous soul and transform it into a house of prayer. You will not become a powerful and anointed Christian who is full of praise and walking in Divine Favor either, unless and until you allow God, by His Holy Spirit, to purify you and transform you into a house of prayer.

Scripture puts this principle as follows: "Then if my people who are called by my name will humble themselves and pray and seek my face and turn from their wicked ways, I will hear from heaven and will forgive their sins and heal their land. I will listen to every prayer made in this place for I have chosen this temple and set it apart to be my home forever. My eyes and my heart will always be here." (2Chronicles 7:14-16 New Living Translation.)

Before we go on to the study the Lord's Prayer, let me be completely candid. If you do not pray, your relationship with

God will not undergo any growth or development. Your relationship will become stagnant. And just like any relationship, if it becomes stale, then soon the friendship dies and the two parties do not spend any time together at all. If you do this with God, you will be in trouble. If you have already made the decision to accept by faith God's gift of salvation, that is the best decision you could ever make. Next, I want to know if you are ready to allow the "LORD" Jesus Christ to be the Lord of your life? If so, I must make this challenge and ask the question: **There is always the pain of choice before the promise of change. So what will it be: the same old routine or are we ready to take the next step with God? Jesus is waiting for us to pray, "Lord, make my temple a house of purity, power, and perfected praise for Your glory." He is ready to begin that divine progression in your temple right now, are you? If so . . . let's go.**

Review the above material very carefully. If you are ready

to move to the next level with God, turn the page.

## Why the Lord's Prayer?

For those of you who are Bible students, you will immediately agree that prayer was a priority for Jesus. With respect to the beginning of His ministry, the Gospel of Mark says that early in the morning, Jesus would go to a quiet and private place to pray. (See Mark 1:35). With respect to the middle of Jesus' ministry, (which is just after He miraculously fed the 5,000), Matthew 14:23 says that Jesus went up alone into the mountain to pray. With respect to the end of Jesus' earthy ministry, Luke's Gospel says that Jesus left the city and, as was his **habit,** he went to pray (Luke 22:39-41).

Prayer was a habit for Jesus and He taught others to pray by His words and example. In the Gospels we discover that the most critical work Jesus did (not including His work on the cross), was to pray. Also, you will notice that almost always after the prayer, Jesus, filled with anointing, compassion, and the power of God, went from those places of prayer to receive the fruits of the battles that he had won in prayer. The fruit of Jesus prayer life was amazing miracles, precise revelations from the Father, spectacular and complete healing of all sorts of diseases, and deliverance from demons and even death. Because prayer was a habit of His life, it is not surprising that even as He faced the taunts and curses from his haters who stood at the foot of the cross, the first words that Jesus spoke as He hung from the cross were a prayer. Jesus said: "Father forgive them for they know not what they do." (See Luke 23:34)

Jesus faced death in the same way that he faced life: unafraid. As he died, Jesus committed His spirit to His Heavenly Father when He declared, "It is finished." (John 19:30). Interestingly enough, most of us think that Jesus' death on the cross marked the end of His prayer ministry. The book of Hebrews says that Jesus' ministry in heaven today is a ministry of prayer. "Wherefore, he [Jesus] is able also to save them to the uttermost that come unto God by him [Jesus], seeing [Jesus] ever liveth to make intercession for them." (Heb 7:25 KJV). (Intercession means prayers for others). In heaven, Jesus is continuing his ministry of prayer and guess what, you are on his prayer list!

The disciples, having seen how prayer produced power and peace throughout Jesus' life and ministry, wanted to know from Jesus how they too could tap into the power of prayer. Interestingly enough, the disciples never asked Jesus to teach them how to preach, but they did ask Him to teach them how to pray. In response to their question, Jesus instructed His disciples, (including us), when you pray, do it like this:

"Our Father which art in heaven, Hallowed be thy name. Thy kingdom come. Thy will be done in earth, as it is in heaven Give us this day our daily bread. And forgive us our debts, as we forgive our debtors. And lead us not into temptation, but deliver us from evil; For Thine is the kingdom, and the power, and the glory, forever." (Matt 6: 9-13) KJV

What I have discovered and what I want to share with you in the next section of this book is an interpretation of the Lord's Prayer. Brad Young, the author of *The Jewish background to the Lord's Prayer* states that the first century Rabbis usually taught by giving topics of truths. They listed certain topics and then under each topic, the rabbis provided a complete outline. In the Lord's Prayer, Rabbi Jesus laid out the topics. That is what He meant when he said, when you pray, do it like this.

Most have memorized, quoted, and sung the Lord's Prayer, but have not seen or been taught the prayer as a group of six topics to follow in prayer under the guidance of the Holy Spirit. What I have learned through much study and prayer is some of the details which fall under each topic. Together, we are going to learn how to pray according to our Lord's will and His word!

Are you ready for the teaching? Good, Chapter 3 will begin the journey.

## Chapter 3

# Do you know His Name?

1) Our Father, who art in Heaven, Hallowed be thy Name!

This is the first topic. The first phrase in the Lord's Prayer tells you that God is our father and that you should be so intimate in your relationship that you can honor our father by calling Him by name. In fact, you are not just supposed to call Him by name, you are instructed to hallow, or declare that His name is holy and worthy of praise. **Remember, prayer is a relationship. All successful relationships have one thing in common; the people involved spend time with each other so that they can get to know each other!** That is why it is so important to begin prayer by establishing the nature and profundity of the relationship that you have with our Heavenly Father. The way that we do this by calling Him by His name!

The very first thing that people do when they start getting to know one another is learn each other's name. But before you can call Him by His name you have to know His name. Do you know His name?

You did not forget to bring your Bible did you! If you don't have your Bible, please go and get it. Remember, you will need it every time you use this book.

Good, now please turn your Bible to Psalm 100. Read the entire Psalm at least twice. Look at verse 4. It says that we are to "enter into His gates with thanksgiving and into his courts with praise," we are to "be thankful unto him and **to bless his name.**" (Psalm 100:4). The first thing that we must do as we enter into prayer is to establish our relationship as we call on God by name.

## *Our Father*

We know from Jesus that we are to call God, "Our Father." It is very important that you understand why. I have come to understand the importance of calling God "Our Father." I want you to memorize the following phrase: **Grace says "our" and faith says "Father!"**

Let me explain "Father" first and then the "Our." We know that because of the work of Jesus, we have the opportunity to have an intimate and personal relationship with God. Jesus' sacrifice for our sins paved the way for us to have access to a personal relationship with God. Each one of us is to recognize that because of Christ, we have been adopted into God's family; He is our Father and we are His children.

God wants to be a father to us in the classic sense of the word. He wants to provide for us and to protect us. He wants to be present with us at all of the significant and even the insignificant moments of our lives. He wants to smile like a proud Father in the delivery room when we are born again and come fresh from the womb of His Spirit. He wants to be the proud Father who boasts as we take our first steps. He wants to be there as we venture out into this life. He wants to comfort us when we stumble; to advise us when we are confused; to play with us and laugh with us and even to correct us when we are wrong. He wants to be our Father. Jesus wants us to know that our Father loves us so much that he wants to be intimate part of our lives.

As we come to know God, we begin to accept by faith that God's desire to be intimate with us is true. We learn from Jesus that Our Father went to great lengths to find us and build a relationship with us. Even before we know that God is our Father, He is our Father. When we come to know this, Jesus says that we should enter into God's presence with the same boldness, access, freedom, and respect that a child would use when he or she comes to his earthly father.

Now some of you who are reading this will say, "Pastor Jones, I did not have a good father. My relationship with my dad was abusive and hurtful. He was not there for me. He did not provide for me or protect me. He never said that he was proud of me and he never corrected me when I was wrong. My father was horrible." If this is your situation, I am sorry for your experience. However, please allow me to encourage you. The Bible teaches that "even if my father and mother abandon me, the Lord will hold me close." (Psalm 27:10 New

Living Translation.) Remember, we come to know God as "our Father" by faith.

Think of all of the things that you wanted your father to be and to do! Imagine what the best father in the world would look like in your eyes. Understand how much He would love you and provide for you and teach you and do for you! Can you imagine? Well, God is all of that and even more that you could ever ask or imagine. Accept by faith that God is your perfect heavenly father. God wants to hold you close and love you like no other. God wants to put you on His lap and encourage you. He wants to be up close and personal with you.

What a tremendous revelation. God wants to get personal with you and he wants you to get personal with Him! He wants you to call him daddy.

Remember our little phrase: **grace says "Our" and faith says "Father."** So what about the "our" in the phrase our father?

The "our" helps to keep us in check. God does not just want to be my Father. He does not just want to be your father. He wants to be everyone's Father. And just like I said a moment ago, even when we don't acknowledge God as Our Father, according to the Word, that does not change the reality that He is our Father. Grace says "our" because the "our" keeps us from forgetting all of our brothers and sisters in this world. Do you realize that if God is "OUR" Father that every human being in the world is our brother or sister (in the spirit that is). This is true even if the brother or sister is not a Christian. This is true no matter what their race, or national origin. This is true no matter what. God loves this entire world and He gave his Son Jesus to die for everyone. Even if others don't accept Jesus, we are still to love them as sisters and brothers. Before we accepted Him, God loved us! We must never be arrogant or haughty because of our personal relationship with God through Jesus Christ. It was all a work of God's grace. We did nothing to earn it and we don't deserve it. God is just that good!

This means that the God who unites us is greater than everything which divides us. This lets us know that God **loves** all of us and that we must be careful about how we treat our sisters and brothers when we approach Our Father.

What I mean by careful is that when we approach **Our** Father, we should not be quick to condemn our brothers and sisters in the presence of Our Father. Never forget that God is not just your Father, He is Our Father. John 3:16 states that "God" so loved the world that he gave his only begotten son, that whosoever believeth on him should not perish but have everlasting life." The bible also teaches that we are saved by GRACE through FAITH and not of works so that no person can brag or boast. Faith makes Him Father but grace makes Him OUR Father.

**Let me be perfectly clear:** *We are able to call God Our Father because of the Blood of the Lord Jesus Christ shed for our sins. When we realize what God has done for us through the sacrifice of Jesus then our spirit cries out to God and declares thank you for adopting us; for making us your children and your heirs. Thank you for being our Father.*

Before we conclude this first section, stop and thank God that He is your Father and that you are His child. Thank God that He loved us enough to send his son, Jesus to find us and to show us the way back home. Good!

Now, let's answer a few review questions before we continue:

**Review:**

1) It is important to honor God when we pray because prayer is a relationship. The way that we enter into the presence of God and honor him is to call God by _____.

2) Psalm 100:4 says: enter into His gates with thanksgiving and into his courts with praise; be thankful unto him and to bless his _____.

3) Jesus wants us to know that God wants to be our _____.

4) We are able to call God Father because of the _____ of the Lord Jesus Christ, shed for our sins.

5) Grace says _____ and faith says _____!

## Hallowed be Thy Name

Now that you are aware that God is "OUR FATHER" and that all of us are brothers and sisters, when you call on Our Father, you are calling on the One who loves us all. No more selfish "me only" prayers, because you are calling on Our Father.

The rest of the phrase says "hallowed be thy name." This means that you are to praise the name of our God. Therefore, simply knowing that God is our Father is not enough. It is just the beginning. If you are going to enter into an intimate relationship with God we have got to know God's name. Father is a title but it is not a name. We come to realize that God is our Father because of our experience with Jesus and His sacrifice on the cross but we learn God's names from our personal and community experiences of the presence of God. The reality of the presence of God is found in the Bible, in the Church, and in the individual experiences of everyday people.

Let me explain what I mean. Take your Bible and read Exodus chapter 3.

*Don't short change yourself. You should know by now that I really want you to read the passage.*

In the passage Moses has an encounter with God in the form of a burning bush. In the encounter, Moses is called by God to lead the people of Israel out of Egypt. As Moses and God go back and forth in the conversation, Moses declares that he needs to know the name of this God if he is going to be able to be effective on his mission. The response from God is that my name is "I AM THAT I AM." In English, this name is often translated Yahweh or Jehovah. Moses learns this Divine Name out of his personal experience with God. Moses is essentially saying, 'before I can go for you, I need to know more about you. I need to know your name.' This is significant because in Bible times because a person's name describes the person's nature. If you know someone's name, you know who they are and what they are really about. Moses needs to know that this God who is calling him is able to help him achieve what he has been called to do. What I like about this divine encounter is that God responds with the ultimate name. The name Jehovah actually means: I am whoever, and whatever I need to be at any time that I need to be it.

The name Jehovah is the basic Biblical name that God gives to Himself. This is the primary place where we find God declaring a name for Himself. Please don't miss the power of God's name. This is one of the most important principles that you will learn as we journey together into prayer. Do you realize that God is telling Moses that He is whatever He needs to be for whatever situation Moses faces!

Are you beginning to see why we need to know His Name?

Let me share other examples with you from the Bible. Next, turn in your Bible to Genesis Chapter 22.

In this passage we find the account of Abraham and God's command for him to offer his son Isaac as a sacrifice to God. God requires Abraham to take his only son and to use him as a burnt offering to God on the mountain. When Abraham and Isaac get to the mountain, Abraham prepares an altar, ties his only son on that altar and lifts a knife preparing to kill his son when the Angel of the Lord shows up. The Angel declares that God has been honored by Abraham's willingness to offer that which he loved most in this world to God. The Angel then shows Abraham that there is a ram caught in the nearby bushes and that this ram will be an adequate sacrifice unto God. The ram becomes a substitute for Isaac and Abraham rejoices. At this point in the story, in verse 14, we find the following words: "And Abraham called the name of the place **Jehovah-jireh**: as it is said to this day. In the mount of the Lord it shall be seen." (Genesis 22:14 KJV)

In this verse you find that Abraham calls the name of the place **Jehovah (or Yahweh – which means I am that I am, or I am whatever I need to be when I need to be it) – jireh. jireh in Hebrew means tangible, visible, provisions.** Therefore, Jehovah-jireh becomes a name for God, which Abraham learns from his personal experience with God. He calls God by His name and declares that in this situation God's provision was seen in the tangible form of a ram in the bush.

Do you begin to see the pattern?

Based on Abraham's personal experience with God, he discovers that God can be called by the name Jehovah-jireh or the Lord who provides for us in a tangible way.

There are at least six other names in the Bible where Jehovah or Yahweh is paired up with some defining characteristic of God. Each of these names comes from either the personal or community experience of God's people with God.

I will list the names and the passages of Scripture where they can be found, take time out right now and read some or all of these passages. The names and corresponding passages are as follow:

**Jehovah-tisdkenu** (sid-kay'-noo): This name means the Lord is my righteousness and is found in Jer. 23: 1-6 verse 6.

**Jehovah-m'kaddesh** (ma-kah'desh)**:** This name means the Lord who sanctifies you and is found in Lev, 20 1-9 particularly verse 8.

**Jehovah-shammah** (sham'mah): This name means the Lord is there and is found in Eze. Chapter 48 particularly the last verse; verse 35.

**Jehovah-shalom** (sha-lom'): This name means the Lord is my/our peace and is found in Phil. 4:1-7.

**Jehovah-rophe** (ro'phay): This name means the Lord heals and is found in Exodus 15:20-27 particularly verse 26.

**Jehovah-jireh** (yeer'a): This name means the Lord's provisions shall be seen and is found in Genesis chapter 22, especially verse 14.

**Jehovah-nissi** (nis'-see): This name means the Lord is my banner, or the Lord goes before me in battle and can be found in Exodus 17:15.

**Jehovah-rohi** (ro'ee): This name means the Lord is my shepherd and can be found in Psalm 23, particularly verse 1.

Remember, what we are talking about is hallowing or praising God's name. We are to praise God because of who He is and because of what He has done for us. Honoring and praising God's name is the biblical means to accessing the presence of God. This is how you are to approach God in prayer. Remember that psalm 100 teaches us to enter into His gates with thanksgiving and into his courts with praise; that we are to be thankful to God and to bless His name.

So, before you set aside time for prayer, take some time to think about who God is or has been in your life and then begin to meditate on that name. As you meditate on the various names of God that you are learning in this chapter, begin to affirm your faith by turning your thoughts into declarations of faith and praise.

For example:

**1) Father, you are Jehovah-tisdkenu. You are my righteousness. I stand before you righteous and forgiven because of the blood of Jesus Christ. I don't have to deal with the guilt of my sins anymore because You have taken my guilt away. Thank you for being my righteousness**

**2) You are Jehovah-m'kaddesh, the Lord who sanctifies. You are conforming me into the image of your Son, Jesus Christ, and breaking sin's power over me. It is because of you that I am able to change and become the person that you want me to be.**

**3) You are Jehovah-shalom; you are my peace. I thank you for filling me with your presence and your Holy Spirit. I thank you because you will never leave me nor forsake me. Thank you for living in and through me, Lord. Because**

**of your love, I live in the peace of God which passes all understanding.**

This is an example of what it means to hallow or praise God by name.

The names that I provided above come from scripture and from our collective benefits as Christians. There are other names as well. For example, in African-American tradition we often hear God referred to as "a heart fixer and a mind regulator." Sometimes, God is referred to as "a way out of no way." Some call Him a "doctor in a sick room and a lawyer in a court room." These names come from the collective and personal experience of Black Americans. From slavery through Jim Crow segregation and racism, God has been all of these and more to African Americans. It is perfectly fine to use whatever name is real for you. The ones from Bible should be real for every Christian; however, you can praise God by calling on any name that describes the great things that God has done just for you as well. As you count your blessings you will discover new names for your heavenly father and your praise will grow and your relationship with God will improve.

For some, he will be your restorer after a great loss. For others, His name will be friend when you are lonely. Others may call him strength to keep on keeping on. Whatever God has been to you, make sure you call Him by name.

There is another verse of scripture that I must share with you as we prepare to close this chapter. The psalm writer declared: Oh magnify the Lord with me. Let us exalt His name together. (Psalm 34:3 KJV). There is a treasure for the believer in this one verse of scripture. One way to understand the idea of magnification is to make something appear bigger than it actually is so that you can see what was there all along but invisible to the naked eye. King David, author of this psalm, is teaching us an important principle in this one verse. I believe that David is telling us that the bigger we make God, the more of God we will be able to see. This portion of the verse suggests that we begin to praise God for what we cannot see. He continues and states that we should exalt His name together. Essentially, the verse is telling you to see our God as Jehovah-(I am whatever you need me to be) and then insert whatever name you need in advance of the need. As you begin to praise God publicly for being what you need in advance, I believe that when you do that, God will become whatever you need, just like His name promises.

What do you need God to be in your life? If you need joy, declare that God is your joy and call God that by name. If you need support, declare that God is your support and call God that by name. If you are in a financial bind and need financial help, declare that God is bigger than your bills and financial burdens. Name him as your provider and the source of your resources and believe me, God will make a way in your life. Your heavenly father will not let you down! He loves you too much to leave you alone and He will make good on all of His promises.

You may not see anything happen immediately. You may not get the answer that you want in the way that you want it. But rest assured that God will answer and will work all things together for your good.

This is how you begin your time with God in prayer. You should not be focusing on your problems but focusing on your God. As problems come to your mind while you are honoring your heavenly father, find a name for God that is bigger than your problems and tell that problem that your heavenly father will supply all of your needs and then hallow

Him by that name. Literally praise God that He is whatever you need!

This is a lot of information to absorb! You might be feeling a little overwhelmed. If so, that is O.K. Just stop and praise God that you have actually made it to this point. That alone is a blessing. Now, if you are feeling pretty good about all that you have read, great! You can stop right now and review by thinking about the great things God has done for us through His Son, Jesus. Praise God for the benefits that He has provided us. Thank Him that because of Jesus' death, burial and resurrection you are no longer a slave to sin. Praise God because He has made us a temple for His Holy Spirit sanctifying us for His presence. Praise God because by His stripes, we are healed. Thank God that we are no longer cursed because of our failure to meet the standard of the Law, but are made righteous by our faith in the Lord Jesus Christ. Praise Him for eternal security, freedom from death and hell and a home in heaven with Him! I am excited because sin no longer stains me, handicaps no longer hinder me, failures no longer frustrate me, difficulties no longer defeat me, death no longer destroys me, and the grave can't keep my body in the ground! – (In case you cannot tell, I am getting excited writing this.) You keep praising God and answer the review questions and we will meet again in the next chapter.

## Review

Go back through this chapter and identify each of the following compound names for God found in the Bible.

**Jehovah-tisdkenu** means _____

**Jehovah-m'kaddesh** means _____

**Jehovah-shammah** means _____

**Jehovah-shalom** means _____

**Jehovah-rophe** means _____

**Jehovah-jireh** means _____

**Jehovah-nissi** means _____

**Jehovah-rohi** means _____

Do you now see that we could spend quite a bit of time in prayer just hallowing the names of our heavenly Father? (This is a yes or no question. If you answered no, then you do not understand. Call your pastor and ask for assistance.)

Very good! Now, are you ready for "Thy Kingdom come, Thy will be done, in earth as it is in heaven?" If so, turn the page and get ready for the next level! It just gets better!

## Chapter 4

# Get Your Priorities Straight

P riorities are very important if one is to be successful in life. The following quote is anonymous yet it powerfully states the power of priorities.

*"What comes first, the compass or the clock? Before one can truly manage time (the clock), it is important to know where you are going, what your priorities and goals are, in which direction you are headed (the compass). Where you are headed is more important than how fast you are going. Rather than always focusing on what's urgent, learn to focus on what is really important."*

Essentially, priorities have two dimensions. First are goals. You have to know where you want to go, or what you want to accomplish before you set out, or odds are you will never get there. Someone once said, "If you fail to plan, you plan to fail."

From a Biblical perspective, goals could be called vision. Biblically, vision is connected to your dreams; your aspirations. A person without vision; without dreams or goals, is a person without direction. Any person without direction is lost. The book of Proverbs expresses this truth in the following manner: "Without a vision, the people perish, but blessed is he who delights in the Law of the Lord." (Proverbs 29:18)

The second essential element in priorities is motivation. Having a goal and no energy or drive to move toward that goal, is a problem. Many of us set goals and have dreams but most of us never actually work toward achieving them.

This is true in everyday life, and is equally true in our spiritual life. If we are going to be successful in our relationship with God and in our everyday dealings with one another, then we must establish heavenly priorities. Establishing heavenly priorities means developing Godly goals or visions, and building the motivation to move toward them. This is what Jesus wants us to do before the Lord.

When Jesus sets out this second topic in prayer he says; "Thy kingdom come; Thy will be done in earth as it is in heaven." In the Greek, what Jesus is literally saying is this: Kingdom of God, come! Will of God, be done on or in earth in the same manner as done in heaven. Jesus wants us to make our number one priority the kingdom of God. This phrase of the Lord's Prayer is written in the imperative mode. This is not a question, it is a declaration.

Turn in your Bible to Matthew 6: 24-33. Stop and read these verses over several times. This is important material and we need to understand it. Jesus says that there are any number of things which could be our number one priority but there is only one thing that should be number one.

In this passage, Jesus teaches that there cannot be two number ones. It creates a conflict. Each thing or person which is number one will compete for your loyalties and trust. Eventually you will have to choose. This is the way life is.

Jesus continues and states that most of the things that people put first are things that they cannot control. He suggests that for all of our efforts, if we make our lives and our body's number one, we cannot control the outcome.

You can do as much as you want to stay healthy, and you should, but you cannot control illness. For all of your worrying, you cannot keep out of harm's way. In essence, what Jesus is teaching is that nothing in this life is certain but God. Seeking after life, or people, or things, may or may not bring the things that you seek. Seeking after God, however, will get you everything that you need to be a success in life.

That is what Jesus means in verse 33. "But seek ye first the kingdom of God and his righteousness; and all these things shall be added unto you."

Do you get it?

If we seek the kingdom, then we don't have to worry about the other issues of life because God promises to take care of our needs.

The important question to be asked now is; what is the Kingdom of God and where can I find it?

Turn in your Bible to Romans chapter 14 and verse 17. Here Paul helps us by telling us what the kingdom of God is. He says: "For the kingdom of God is not meat or drink; but righteousness, and peace, and joy in the Holy Ghost." (KJV). This is a verse that you should memorize if you can. If not, at least highlight it in your Bible and make a note of where you can find it.

Permit me a moment to expound on this verse because it might help you understand better what the Kingdom of God is and what it means to seek it first!

## *What is the Kingdom?*

Paul wants us to know that the Kingdom of God is not based on things. You cannot tell that you are in the Kingdom because you are blessed with great material wealth, health, or strength. For the Kingdom of God is **NOT** meat or drink. It is not based on material blessings. Rather, the Kingdom of God is righteousness, joy and peace in the Holy Ghost.

What does that mean? Good question.

It means the Kingdom of God is that reality where the Holy Spirit is in complete control. It is that reality where God's will and purpose are the only order of the day. It is a reality where things occur on earth just as they occur in Heaven. By this, I do not mean to imply that there are no more tears and no more trouble. Instead, I mean that the will of God is done perfectly.

Paul describes the Kingdom by saying that it is righteousness. When Paul states that the Kingdom of God is righteousness he means that people who are living according to the Kingdom reality are always trying to do the right thing. As a practical reality, Paul is teaching us that as people begin to know the will of God, they simply do it. Righteousness simply means to do the right thing.

Paul also describes the Kingdom as a reality of joy. What his message suggests here is that persons of the Kingdom find joy in simply doing the will of God. They are convinced that God is preparing them, and has prepared a place of safety and security for them. They understand that no matter what the earthly situation or problem, God is their strength, power, friend, protector, comforter, guide, leader, shepherd, redeemer, deliverer, and savior. They know that come what may, from day to day, God will take care of them. Kingdom Joy is not based on our ability to control our circumstances. To the contrary, Kingdom joy knows that we are not in control, but God is. Kingdom minded people can find joy even when everything around them is uncomfortable, ugly, sick, and dying. Now that is joy.

Next Paul describes the kingdom as a place of peace. By peace, he means a sense of well-being and wholeness whereby the person of the Kingdom is confident, secure, stable, and internally calm even in the midst of life's storms. Paul is describing the inner peace which comes when one understands that God has provided them with eternal security.

> **The Kingdom mindset is accomplished by and in the Holy Ghost.**

What Paul really wants us to understand is that the Kingdom is a state of mind. It is a way of thinking, which translates into a way of living. Jesus teaches us that the Kingdom of God is within us. What he means is that we must know the will of God for ourselves and then be willing to do it. When we understand that God's will is always the best thing for us, we can find joy even in sorrow and peace even in the face of great confusion. So, the Kingdom of God begins in our minds by us studying to show ourselves approved unto God such that we can be workers who do not need to be ashamed. (See 1 Tim. 2:15)

Jesus wants our number one priority in life to be to live in that reality where we are subject to the perfect will of God. He wants our mindset to be one in which we always try to do what God wants us to do and where we seek God's joy and peace in life regardless of what comes our way. Therefore, Christ teaches, seek ye first the Kingdom of God and His righteousness, and all these things will be added unto you!

> *How do we become Kingdom citizens*
> *before we reach heaven?*

When we are saved; when we accept Christ as our personal savior; we enter into the Kingdom. However, that does not mean that we live as Kingdom citizens now. Accepting Christ ensures us a place in heaven after this life but it does not guarantee that we will experience the reality of the Kingdom before we cross over into eternity. Jesus says that we must make a positive affirmation and then begin to walk by faith in our affirmation.

Let me explain:

He says that we should pray Kingdom of God come! Will of God be done on or in earth, as it is done in heaven. What Jesus wants us to do is to declare daily that to the best of our ability and by the power of the Holy Ghost, we will be Kingdom citizens right now. He wants us to declare that this day, we will always do that which is right and pleasing in God's sight; that we will experience Joy in our journey because we will walk with God by His Spirit; and that we can be confident that come what may, everything will be ok. Jesus wants us to declare before God that with His help, the Kingdom of God will be our reality, and that the perfect will of God will be our will.

Now, when you pray this part of the prayer, you should affirm and declare that you will have a Kingdom mindset for **yourselves** all day. Then you should pray for that same mindset in your **family**. Prayer for your family should include your spouse, parents, brothers, and sisters, and any other family member that God places on our hearts while we are praying.

Next, you should pray for your **Church.** You should declare that the leadership and membership of the Church would experience a kingdom mindset and a kingdom reality every day. After you pray for your local congregation, you should pray for **all Churches** and their leadership and membership. **In so doing, you, your families, and God's church will begin to experience the power** of the **Kingdom of God** in **their** individual and collective lives.

Finally, you should pray for **your city, your nation, and this world.** You should pray for presidents, officials, political and economic leaders, world leaders and governments and declare - not beg or ask - but declare that the Kingdom will be their mindset and reality and that the will of God will be their will every day.

Can you imagine what would happen if everyone in your local church prayed just this part of the Lord's Prayer every day! Our church, our families, our personal lives, and our cities would begin to be transformed into a place where righteousness would become normal. Crime, sin, violence, anger, and frustration would decrease and joy and peace in the Holy Ghost would increase. We really need to pray!

The benefits of this section of Jesus model of prayer are beyond measure. When we make the Kingdom of God our priority, God makes our needs His priority. The benefit is magnified when we pray this prayer for our families, friends and community. As we come together in agreement and pray

Kingdom of God come; Will of God be done; souls will be saved, lives will be changed and God will be glorified.

**\* Review**

1) Jesus teaches that we can only have one #1 priority. According to Jesus our #1 priority should be _____ of God.

2) According to Paul, the Kingdom of God is not meat or drink but righteousness and _____ and _____ in the Holy _____.

3) The Kingdom of God is not measured by materialism. Rather the Kingdom of God is an attitude or a state of _____.

4) When we pray Thy Kingdom come, Thy will be done, we should declare before God that the Kingdom will be a reality

and God's will, will be the will of ourselves, our family, our

_____, all _____, our city, our nation, and our

world.

5) When we pray this prayer, we should not beg, rather we
should make a faith statement or simply _____ that the
kingdom is our reality by the help of God.

Stop right now and take a few minutes to practice. Declare
before God that with His help, you will have a kingdom
mindset right now. Declare that you will know what is right
and will do the right thing. Declare that you will be able
to find joy regardless of what happens today and that you
have peace because of your confidence that the perfect will
of God will be done this day. Make the same declaration for
your family, your church, all churches, your city, your nation,
and this world! Praise God. When you finish praying, we are
ready to move on to the next teaching in the Lord's Prayer.
Turn the page and get ready for the next lesson.

## Chapter 5

# Our Daily Bread

I n Jesus' model prayer you should begin to see a pattern unfolding. You begin by entering into the presence of God by calling Him by name. Then you establish your priorities in His presence by declaring: Kingdom of God come and will of God be done. Next, you begin to talk to God about your needs and it is here that you will learn some powerful truths about God's provision. Jesus says that when you pray you should say: "Give us this day our daily bread."

In biblical days bread was one of the symbolic words which represented life. This was so was because bread was a part of everyone's diet. It was something that everyone in Palestine ate every day. If you did not have bread, you did not have the most basic of foods. In Bible days a person without bread would not live very long. Therefore, bread was considered the staff of life.

This same idea made its way into American society. There was a time when we in America used to call money bread. The reason why is because Americans knew that a person who did not have any money would not live very long in this world. If you do not have money, you cannot acquire the basic necessities of life. Think about how life would change if tomorrow someone took away all of your money and shut the door of opportunity so that you could not earn any more. If you or I found ourselves in this situation, we would be in an extremely difficult position. Before long the bank or the landlord would put us out of our homes. Our creditors would come and repossess our belongings. We would be unable to purchase food or clothes. In that situation, none of us would last for very long. We would either have to become thieves and steal to eat or we would have to depend on the charity of others. We might even die trying to provide for ourselves by taking foolish and dangerous risks. There are certain basics that we all need if we are going to be able to live in this world. Now I am not talking about luxuries and extras at this point. I am talking about basics. I am talking about bread.

Social scientists state that every human being needs at least three things: food, shelter, and companionship. I don't know whether you want to believe the scientists but I tell you that none of us would live for very long in the absence of any of the above. Try living without food. No one can last for too long without food to sustain them. Try making it through the winter without shelter. If you have no place to lay your head and no place to be warm in the cold, the cold will kill you. Try making it in this world all by yourself with no one to encourage you, no one to raise you, and no one to hold your hand when you are afraid and alone. Without these three basics you would not be able to live for very long.

Unfortunately, too many of us are living our lives trying to acquire the things that we want and are dying on the inside because we don't have the things that we need. When it comes to the basics most of us are in trouble. For example, the vast majority of us would rather eat hearty than eat healthy. Many of us would rather live in the lap of luxury than live in a home where people actually care for one another. We want to have a castle full of possessions that we can't even use, rather than living in a home where the members of a family know and love each other. And when it comes to companionship, we all claim that we want it, but too many of us are unwilling to do what it takes to have it. Some of us don't have any friends because we don't know how to be a friend. We are too busy looking out for number one.

So what does all of this have to do with prayer?

Wonderful question!

Jesus is trying to tell us that when we pray we need to ask God for our daily bread. He is saying that we need to ask God to help us have our basic spiritual and physical needs met. He is saying that we need to ask God to give us food, shelter, and companionship.

In Chapter 1 of John's Gospel the following is recorded:

"In the beginning was the word and the word was with God and the word was God." (John 1:1 KJV)

John goes on to say that the word became flesh and dwelt among us. That word is Jesus. In John chapter 6, we learn that Jesus declared that he is the bread of life!

When we put these two biblical truths together, we come to understand that there are three powerful provisions that God already has for us and we must appropriate them in prayer.

1) What we need is the food that comes from the Word of God.

You clearly need food for your physical body. In the same manner you need food for your spirit. The only place that you can find consistent life giving spiritual food is in the Word of God. You see, Jesus is the Word incarnate and you have direct access to this Word in the form of the Bible. If you do not have a regular diet of Bible in your life then you are spiritually malnourished. Therefore, when you pray give us this day our daily bread, you must ask God to give you a **desire** to study the Word both at church, in Bible class and daily at home. You must ask that God would open up your eyes and ears to understand the message and meaning of that Word. You must then allow that word to nourish and sustain you. In the same manner that God provides physical food for you, He has also provided you with the Bread of Life through the Word of God.

2) We need shelter in the time of storm.

When life's storms begin to rage, you need to know that you have a shelter that will protect you from the elements. Just as you have a physical need for shelter, you also have a spiritual need for shelter. When you eat the Word, and when the Word comes alive in you, you then have an answer, or a shelter, to some of life's great storms. When fear comes in like a flood, you can declare, **God did not give me a spirit of fear, but a spirit of love, power, and a sound mind.**

If people continue to challenge you, attack you, demean you, and seek to destroy you, you can declare, **The Lord is my light and my salvation, whom shall I fear? The Lord is the strength of my life, of whom shall I be afraid?**

When the darkness and loneliness of midnight come to visit your spirit; when you find ourselves in the worst part of your own personal night, you can declare: **Weeping may endure for a night but joy comes in the morning.**

When you constantly hear from others or even in your own mind the words: "You can't. You can't. You can't achieve it, you can't have it, you can't make it!" - Then you can rise up and declare that **you can do all things through Christ who strengthens you.**

You need God's provision of shelter in the time of storm. The shelter that I speak of only comes when you know the Word of God. If you fail to study the Word, feed on the Word, and allow the Word to live in you then you will be spiritually homeless and defenseless in the time of storm.

3) We need God's provision of companionship.

God promises in the Word that he will never leave you or forsake you. He promises that when people don't understand you or your faith; when friends forsake you because of your religion; when changes come in your life and you don't do what you used to or go where you used to; that He (God) will go with you. God promises to be with you and that the Word will provide comfort and companionship for you. The Word helps you understand that you are not alone. No matter where you go and no matter what you do, God promises in the word that He will be with you. When the Word is in you, wherever you are, the Word is there also.

So when you pray "Give us this day our daily bread," you should be asking God to give you the desire, the energy, the determination, and the faith to study the Word, to learn the meaning of the Word. You should ask God to help you to memorize passages in the Word, to strengthen you from the Word, to provide shelter for you with the Word, and to make the Word be your constant companion!

Remember, in Jesus' model of prayer, you can never be selfish. As you ask God to meet your needs, you are not finished until you ask the same for your family, friends, church, community, nation and world. Not only is your prayer life critical to meeting your needs, but you have a role to play in meeting the needs of the entire world. You are a Kingdom Citizen and this is a fundamental part of your responsibility. Your prayers have tremendous power . . . if you pray.

**Review**

1) Provisions are not our wants. When we speak of provisions, we are speaking of basic human _____.

2) There are three basic human needs that social scientists tell us that we all need. They are _____, _____, and _____.

3) All of our basic needs are met through the _____ of God.

Hopefully, you are beginning to see that God's Word will sustain and nurture your spirit. If you do not understand that the Word of God is life, then your life will never be fulfilled. Take 5 minutes now to ask God to open your heart to the Word, to fill your thoughts with the Word, to feed you from the Word, to shelter you in the Word, and to provide companionship for you from the Word.

Good. Now, turn the page and let's look at the next lesson.

## Chapter 6

# Forgiveness Is Not Optional

O ne of the most interesting powers granted to the President of the United States, to heads of states of other countries, and the Governors of the 50 states is the power to grant pardons. What is unique about this power is that the President or Governor is aware that the person requesting pardon is guilty of all charges. The one asking for the pardon actually committed the offense and deserves the punishment that has been meted out to them. They have no excuse. They have exhausted every appeal and have been justly sentenced. Even with all of the evidence and judgment against them, the President or Governor has the right to completely forgive the offense and set aside the sentence.

In order to receive a pardon and you must do three simple things. First, you must have been convicted of a crime. Second, you must ask for the pardon for yourself. Third, you must be willing to accept the terms of the one granting the pardon.

This process is very similar to what Jesus offers in this teaching on prayer. We make our petition to God - "forgive us our debts" - and by doing so, we come to God and acknowledge that we are in debt. Essentially, we must come to God and admit our guilt and ask for a pardon. This phase of the process is tremendously important because it forces us to be honest with ourselves. We cannot come to God with a sense of arrogance or entitlement. Instead, we come to God with an attitude of humility and apology. We come with regret and a spirit of repentance. We come believing that we need a pardon and that God is gracious enough to offer it to us.

We are able to come to God with this confidence on the basis of His Word. 1 John 1:8-9 states: *If we claim we have no sin, we are only fooling ourselves and not living in the truth. But if we confess our sins to him, he is faithful and just to forgive us our sins and to cleanse us from all wickedness.* (The New Living Translation). This powerful verse of scripture makes is clear that if we admit our sins to God and ask for forgiveness, we have every right to expect that a Divine Pardon is not only possible but available. We are promised forgiveness and the power to be cleansed from all of the guilt, regret and drama that sin always causes. In other words, we are not only forgiven, but all of the debt is paid in full.

At this point you may be fully ready to rejoice in the simple knowledge that you are forgiven and debt free. But remember, Grace says "our" and "faith" says "Father." At this point, you have only addressed the "faith" section of this prayer. You have come to Our Father and only asked for forgiveness for yourself. There is another condition to this pardon. "Forgive us our debts . . . as we forgive our debtors."

Please don't miss the power of this prayer. Jesus teaches that in order to receive your pardon you must be willing to offer the same pardon to those who are in debt to you. What this literally says is that if you don't forgive others, God will not forgive you. If you partially forgive others, God will only partially forgive you. But if you completely forgive others, God will completely forgive you.

Again, look at what the Bible states as Jesus Himself provides commentary on his teaching about forgiveness and prayer:

Matthew 6:14-15 states: *"If you forgive those who sin against you, your heavenly Father will forgive you. But if you refuse to forgive others, your Father will not forgive your sins."* (The New Living Translation)

Let me give you the same verses in The Message Translation: *"In prayer there is a connection between what God does and what you do. You can't get forgiveness from God, for instance, without also forgiving others. If you refuse to do your part, you cut yourself off from God's part."*

When you labor in prayer for pardon, you must understand the conditions. This means that we must be prepared to begin this section of prayer by asking God to help us to pardon others. If we begin this part of the prayer on ourselves first, we run the risk of missing our blessing by messing up our pardon. The sad reality is that many of us come to God for forgiveness and regularly walk away guilty because we fail to fulfill the third requirement. We fail to forgive others first.

Let me provide you with a biblical story that addresses this truth. Take a few moments to read Matthew 18:21-35. I have printed it here in The Message Translation:

"21 At that point Peter got up the nerve to ask, "Master, how many times do I forgive a brother or sister who hurts me? Seven?" 22 Jesus replied, "Seven! Hardly. Try seventy times seven. 23 "The kingdom of God is like a king who decided to square accounts with his servants. 24 As he got under way, one servant was brought before him who had run up a debt of a hundred thousand dollars. 25 He couldn't pay up, so the king ordered the man, along with his wife, children, and goods, to be auctioned off at the slave market. 26 "The poor wretch threw himself at the king's feet and begged, "Give me a chance and I'll pay it all back.' 27 Touched by his plea, the king let him off, erasing the debt. 28 "The servant was no sooner out of the room when he came upon one of his fellow servants who owed him ten dollars. He seized him by the throat and demanded, "Pay up. Now!' 29 "The poor wretch threw himself down and begged, "Give me a chance and I'll pay it all back.' 30 But he wouldn't do it. He had him arrested and put in jail until the debt was paid. 31 When the other servants saw this going on, they were outraged and brought a detailed report to the king. 32 "The king summoned the man and said, "You evil servant! I forgave your entire debt when you begged me for mercy. 33 Shouldn't you be compelled to be merciful to your fellow servant who asked for mercy?' 34 The king was furious and put the screws to the man until he paid back his entire debt. 35 And that's exactly what my Father in heaven is going to do to each one of you who doesn't forgive unconditionally anyone who asks for mercy."

When teaching on forgiveness, Jesus tells Peter and all of us who are listening in that there is a danger in getting forgiven before you consider forgiving others. In fact, this passage makes it clear that forgiving others is critical to receiving our own forgiveness.

The lesson for us here is that when we come to God for pardon, we should begin by asking God to give us the strength and courage to forgive others first. I suggest that you begin by asking God to forgive those who are sexist, racist, homophobic, mean-spirited, bigoted and hateful. You must forgive the damage that their misguided beliefs and wicked behavior have caused **and** you must forgive them. It is important that you don't let the work of the enemy make you bitter. You must be willing to ask God for the grace to forgive the prejudice of others, so that God will forgive the prejudice in you.

Please note that I am not stating that you must condone this behavior, only that you ask God for the grace to forgive those who practice it. I know that is seems impossible for an African American to forgive slavery or for women to forgive sexism, but if we want to be pardoned and powerful, we must. Our greatest chance for deliverance and transformation comes when we beg God for the grace to forgive others.

After dealing with social and systemic issues with a global impact, we must move to more specific situations such as your co-workers, the bully at school, the rude person at the bank or at the store who was offensive toward you. All of these people must be forgiven. The person who cut you off in traffic or who cut you off in conversation, the person who took your parking space or wasted your time, all of these must be forgiven. Again, if you want to be pardoned and powerful in these areas, the prerequisite is that you forgive others.

Then we must bring the circle closer. We must forgive ex-girlfriends and boyfriends; ex-husbands and ex-wives; abusive family members and friends who have hurt us in any number of ways or we will never be pardoned and powerful.

Once we have spent time in prayer asking God to help us to release others, then we can turn our attention to our personal need for forgiveness. Finally, after all of these prerequisites have been met, it is time to address my guilt, my faults, my flaws and my sins. Lord, now that you have empowered me to forgive all of this, please forgive me!

You will discover that the more you get God's grace to forgive others, the more you will walk in the power of God forgiveness for you. Imagine living spiritually debt free! No guilt! No bitterness! No hatred! No revenge! Just free to love and to live! This is the promise of the Pardon of God!

Take a short break and let's pray. Join me as we begin to ask God to grant us the grace to pardon others.

*Father, please help me to release those who have come against You and Your purpose for Your world. Help me to forgive those who choose to be wicked; those who choose to exploit the weak and to hurt and humiliate others. Help me to forgive those who have treated me inappropriately because of my race, age, gender, weight, personality or any other characteristic. Grant me the power to forgive and not to be resentful or vengeful against these principalities and powers.*

*Father, I also ask you to help me to forgive the people that I have or will encounter today. Help me to forgive those who have been rude and ruthless toward me. Help me to forgive those who have hurt me and made my life a living hell. Grant me the grace to release them to you so that you can bless them and heal them.*

*Father, help me to forgive those who are closest to me. Family members, and close friends who knowingly or unknowingly have done me harm are now released into your love and grace. I make up my mind to forgive them and to return love for any offense.*

*Now, Father, I ask you to forgive me. I have sinned against you and stand before you guilty. I ask you to grant me the grace of your forgiveness and that you cleanse me of all of my wicked ways. 1 John 1:9 states that if I confess my sins, You are faithful and just to forgive me of my sins and to cleanse me of all unrighteousness. I now claim that promise and receive your forgiveness and complete healing.*

**Review**:

1) In order to receive a presidential pardon and you must do three simple things. First, you must have been _____ of a crime. Second, you must _____ the pardon for yourself. Third, you must be willing to _____ the terms of the one granting the pardon.

2) Before you can receive God's pardon for your sins, you must first _____ the sins of others

3) According to 1 John 1:9 God promises to forgive you of your sins and to _____ you from all unrighteousness.

Now that you have forgiven others and received God complete forgiveness, turn to the next page and let's go deeper into prayer.

## Chapter 7

# Temptation – Don't Face It Alone

All of us have a need to feel safe. Life has a way of creating situations where safety is uncertain. Sometimes it is internal fears and doubts that cause uncertainty and other times it is external circumstances that produce instability. Either way, we all have to deal with uncertainty, insecurity, and our desire for safety.

In this comprehensive teaching on prayer, Jesus instructs us to focus on both our internal and external safety. He teaches us to come to Our Father and ask for divine protection.

First we are instructed to ask for help with temptation. There is a great hymn of the church that gives us some insight.

Take a few moments to read the lyrics to the hymn: Yield Not
To Temptation:

Verse 1:

Yield not to temptation, for yielding is sin;

each victory will help you some other to win;

fight manfully onward, dark passions subdue,

look ever to Jesus, He'll carry you through.

Verse 2:

Shun evil companions, bad language disdain;

God's name hold in reverence, nor take it in vain;

be thoughtful and earnest, kind-hearted and true;

look ever to Jesus, He'll carry you through.

Verse 3:

To him that o'ercometh, God giveth a crown;

through faith we shall conquer, though often cast down;

He who is our Savior our strength will renew;

look ever to Jesus, He'll carry you through.

Chorus:

Ask the Savior to help you,

comfort, strengthen and keep you;

He is willing to aid you,

He will carry you through.

Temptation is when our appetites drive us to do what our insights know is not good for us. It is those moments when we are struggling with a choice that we know is not good for us, but we want to choose it anyway. Temptations come in every category of our lives; financial, spiritual, emotional, physical, relational, and social. When these moments come, we must be strong enough in our insights that our appetites don't make our choices for us.

Whenever we are driven by hunger and not holiness we will make bad decisions. In essence, the first part of prayer for protection is to ask God to help us to make decisions based on Divine insight and not personal appetite. It is to do what the first verse of the hymn declares: to yield not to temptation for yielding is sin.

When Jesus teaches us to pray lead us not into temptation, he is not telling us to ask God to let us avoid temptation, rather he is telling us to ask God to help us to get the victory over temptation. Every victory strengthens us and gives us a sense of security and safety because it builds our confidence that we can make healthy choices and live healthy lives.

First, we are to ask God to help us to make healthy and holy personal choices. We are asking the Lord to help us to not be driven by our appetites and hunger pains, but to help us to take the driver's seat and choose to move in directions that lead to health, safety and longevity rather than ones that lead to instant gratification, temporary satisfaction and long term danger.

Next we must also do the second verse of the hymn. That begins by asking to make healthy choices in our relationships. The wrong relationships can wreak havoc in ways that are almost beyond measure. Who you marry, who you choose to partner with in business, who you hang out with, can all have a dramatic impact for good or evil in your life.

If you don't make wise choices regarding the relationships in your life, you will constantly be taken advantage of or used by others. Lord, help me not to enter into relationships on the basis of temptation.

Finally, the hymn challenges us to be careful about our language. How often are we tempted to speak negative words into the atmosphere? We must be careful that no matter what the circumstances, we refuse to be tempted to use self-defeating and life destroying language.

Our prayer must be to ask the savior to help us with these three aspects of temptation. Let me review for simplicity.

Lead me not into temptation . . .

1) Help me to make healthy choices in my personal life.

2) Help me to make healthy choices in my relationships.

3) Help me to make healthy choices in my language.

I know that I will be tempted in each of these areas and if I yield to that temptation, I will fail, but if I overcome the temptation, I will get the victory.

Jesus also tells us to ask to be delivered from evil. This is the second aspect of the prayer for protection. Literally, this means that even if we make the best possible choices, we may still end up in a bad situation. When we find ourselves in a battle with evil, we need to be delivered.

Essentially, we are saying Lord, help me to do the best that I can and when my best does not get the victory, I need you to have my back. I know that my best choices may not always lead me to a place of safety and security. I know that evil will never leave me alone and that I will have to struggle. I know that trouble will come. But, in spite of all of that, I know that you are well able to deliver me from all evil. I put my request in to you in advance and I trust you. I am confident that after I have done all that I can do to stand in faith, I can count on you to cover me and see me safely through. I am confident that God will carry me through.

When we know that we have God's promise to protect us in every area of our lives, this gives us a sense of safety and peace of mind that is beyond measure.

I want to encourage you to take five minutes right now to call on God and ask for divine protection. Here is an example:

*Father, I know that I struggle to make good choices. I need your help to keep me from the temptations that come internally and externally. Sometimes I let my appetites and desires drive me to make choices that I know are not in my best interest. Help me to think more and react less. Help me to choose with wisdom and not wishful thinking. Help me to be patient, deliberate, determined and faithful and not impatient, impulsive, shortsighted and foolish. Lord, help me to make wise choices for me personally, relationally and in my communication. Cover me, Lord, with your wisdom and your purpose.*

*Lord, when I do make bad choices, or when things don't seem to be going according to your will. When I find myself stuck and surrounded by evil, I am counting on you to deliver me because I know that I can't deliver myself. I need you!*

*Lord, after you help me, I pray that you will help my family, my friends, my church, my community, my country and your world to have the same protection that you have provided for me. You are a great God and I count on you to keep your promise. You promised to protect your children and I take you at your word! In Jesus' Mighty Name . . . AMEN.*

**Review**

1) Temptation is when our _____ drive us to do what our _____ know is not good for us.

2) Temptation is more about my personal _____. If my choices are poor, then I will yield to temptation and fall into sin.

3) I need God's help with my choices in three areas. They are my _____, my _____ and my language.

4) When I have done the best that I can with my choices, I can count on God to have my back. God promises to _____ me from evil!

If you have taken time to pray and reflect, we have one more chapter to address. Turn the page with me and let's look at what is next . . . .

# Chapter 8

# Send The Praises Up

The final verse of the Lord's Prayer states: For Thine is the kingdom and the power, and the glory, forever, Amen.

It has come to me by reasonably reliable authority that the mark of culture and the stamp of breeding are to be measured by the use of what society calls etiquette. We are characterized as polite or impolite, rude or refined; by our ability or inability to make the proper use of etiquette. Etiquette says that there are certain responses for certain situations. If you ask a favor, it is anticipated that you will preface your plea by the word, "Please." If you make an error, you acknowledge your mistake with the words, "I'm sorry." If you interrupt others, "excuse me." And if somebody does something for you or to you or with you, it is appropriate to say, in response to their kindness, "Thank you." This is the lesson of etiquette.

I bring this lesson to your attention only because we are living in a world that has lost nearly all sense of propriety and order. Very often we don't know what to do, or how to do, or when to do – we just do! People will run over you and never look back to say, "Excuse me." They will ask you for the world and expect you to give it to them and never say the word, "please." Then there are those who will take you and everything about you for granted and never once say, "thank you." Of all the breaches of etiquette, I don't know of one that cuts more deeply or wounds more openly than the failure of a debtor to say, "thank you."

Now you might not have thought about the theological implications of the words "thank you," but I believe there is a spiritual dimension to the discipline of saying it. I am convinced that a sincere and simple thank you is critical to our spiritual well-being and is vital to our prayer life.

Very simply stated, Jesus wants us to know that since God has done so much for us, we should have the decency to say thank you. Anything less is rude and presents a problem to our relationship. Theologically, if we fail to thank God then we are in essence taking the grace of God for granted. Whenever any one party in a relationship takes the other for granted, the relationship is doomed. If we fail to thank God, then we might as well not pray. We must thank Him for the great things He has done, is doing, and will do! Remember; always end your prayer in thanks to God!

Let me provide you with a powerful Biblical example:

Luke 17:11-19 (The Message Translation):

"[11]It happened that as he made his way toward Jerusalem, he crossed over the border between Samaria and Galilee. [12]As he entered a village, ten men, all lepers, met him. They kept their distance [13]but raised their voices, calling out, "Jesus, Master, have mercy on us!"

14Taking a good look at them, he said, "Go, show yourselves to the priests." They went, and while still on their way, became clean. 15One of them, when he realized that he was healed, turned around and came back, shouting his gratitude, glorifying God. [16]He kneeled at

Jesus' feet, so grateful. He couldn't thank him enough--and he was a Samaritan.

[17]Jesus said, "Were not ten healed? Where are the nine? [18]Can none be found to come back and give glory to God except this outsider?" [19]Then he said to him, "Get up. On your way. Your faith has healed and saved you."

Notice in this passage, that all ten of the lepers were healed but only one of them has a powerful and personal relationship with Jesus. All of the men received a blessing but one of the ten received salvation and the only difference between the nine and the one was the simple attitude of gratitude.

Expressing praise and thanks to God ensures that we will receive the fullness of God's favor and the maximum benefit of God's grace. Why, you ask? Well, whenever we are ungrateful, one of two problems arise. Either we have a sense of entitlement or we are taking someone else's kindness for granted. Entitlement means that we think we deserve what we have received from others and therefore are not obligated to say thank you. Taking another's kindness for granted means that what they are doing for us has become so common that we don't think it is a big deal anymore. Either response is dangerous to a relationship and will eventually cause others to pull back in their generosity.

Being thankful is God's will for our lives because God delights in the praises of His people. In fact, I believe that in order to receive all that God has for us; we must give God all of the praise that is due to Him. Praise is actually one of the greatest weapons that the believer has at their disposal.

When we praise God, we activate heaven's resources to come to our aid and the results are tremendous. Closing our time of prayer with an attitude of gratitude and the voice of our praise brings power into our situation and circumstance and enables us to face our spiritual adversary with confidence and assurance. There is one more passage of scripture that you must read before we bring our discussion to a close.

In 2 Chronicles Chapter 20 the story of King Jehoshaphat, a king of Judah, is recorded. In this remarkable story, we find that three nations have come together and decided to attack Jehoshaphat and Judah. When Jehoshaphat gets the word that this massive enemy force has come together to attack him and his people, he and his advisors evaluate the situation and are clear that they don't have the resources or ability to win.

Immediately, King Jehoshaphat commands the entire nation of Judah to fast and pray. Their prayer is powerful and includes all of the aspects of the prayer lesson that Jesus has provided for us. At the close of the prayer, the people wait for God to answer . . . and God does. God speaks and declares that the people of Judah will get the victory. God tells them to go and face their enemies the next day and not to worry because the battle no longer belongs to them, it belongs to Him.

Verses 18 and 19 of Chapter 20 declare that after the prayer and God's answer, the king and all of the people worship and praise God with a loud voice. Then the King and his advisors plan how they will obey God and face their enemies. Recognizing the power of praise, King Jehoshaphat instructs the choir to get together and go out in front of the army. They are given the lyrics to be sung: Hallelujah, His mercy endures forever! As the people line up behind the choir and go towards the enemy the bible teaches that while they were praising, God confuses the enemy armies such that they all kill each other.

By the time Jehoshaphat and the people got to the battle field, all of their enemies were dead, but all of their equipment, resources, and money were all there for the taking. Also, the story ends by declaring that Jehoshaphat and all of Judah lived in peace for the rest of his reign.

The lesson here is profound and powerful for all of us who pray the prayer that Jesus taught us to pray. Here it is . . .

> ***If you want to get the victory, end your prayer with praise!***

I hope that you are beginning to see why prayer is the most important discipline in the development of mature and powerful Christians. The disciples discovered that the key source of Jesus power was prayer. That is why the only things that the disciples asked Jesus to teach them to do is to pray.

For those of you who made it through to the end of this book, let me expose the secret in the clearest possible terms:

> ***The power of God is released in the person with a personal relationship with God and the only way to build a solid personal relationship with God is in PRAYER!***

If you are ready for the power to be released, make this book your constant companion and make prayer your priority. I also ask you to please become a partner in prayer with me.

Because I value the relationship that I have with God, and now with you, I want to express my personal "thank you" to you for purchasing this book. I also want to take time to thank you in advance for praying for me, for your pastor, for your family, for your friends and enemies, for your city, community, country and world.

I am thankful for the privilege of sharing this time and treasure with you! If this book blessed you, please follow me on twitter at <u>www.twitter.com/pastormikejones</u> or on Facebook at <u>www.facebook.com/pastormj</u>. Also, I thank you in advance for sharing this book with others. Please purchase additional copies for friends and loved ones. Please share this book with others if it has been a blessing to you.

Finally, I thank God for the honor of being able to be your prayer pastor and partner. I have made a commitment to pray daily for everyone who touches this book. I know that God loves you and He is waiting for you to come and spend time with Him in Prayer.

God bless you!

With a pastor's heart,

## *Pastor Michael K. Jones, M.Div.*

Senior Pastor, Progressive Baptist Church

4625 W. 49th Street

Indianapolis, In 46254

**Review**

**Prayer outline:**

**1) Enter into the PRESENCE of God by calling on God's name.**

Prayer is about having a personal relationship with God. One of the first things that we do when we meet is exchange names. As you learn the names of God, you will come to know the nature of God and your relationship with take off.

**2) Establish Kingdom PRIORITIES in the Presence of God**

Personal relationships must be a priority. If you want any relationship to be successful, you and the person with whom you desire a relationship must establish priorities together. No goals - no glory! In the case of a relationship with God, you must come to know God's will.

**3) Receive God's PROVISIONS**

In every relationship, there are needs that must be met if the relationship is to be successful. God desires to meet your needs so that the relationship can thrive. You and I have to be honest enough to express our needs to God before we can expect our needs to be met.

### 4) Receive and Extend God's PARON

All relationships have rough patches. If we are not able to forgive, we are not able to live! Unforgiveness is a killer of all relationships. If we can receive forgiveness from God, we can share forgiveness with others.

### 5) Request God's PROTECTION

If we are honest, there are some things in life that we just don't want to endure alone. Because of our personal relationship with God, we can expect not only God's presence, but God's protection along the way. God desires to provide safety and security to all of His family. If you are willing, He is able.

### 6) Express PRAISE to God

What God desires from us is our appreciation and gratitude. This is what we bring to the table that "meets a need" for God. Now, don't think I am confused, God doesn't require our praise but the bible does teach that if we don't praise Him, the rocks will do it in our stead. Praise is dramatically connected to gratitude in that we praise God as our grateful response for all that God has done for us.

Finally, please remember that every area of prayer is designed to be personal and portable. We are to pray not only for ourselves, but we are also to pray for our family, our church, our community, our country and even our world.

If you spend hours in every section of the Lord's teaching on prayer but just pray for yourself, your prayers will be ineffective. Critical to success in prayer is that you engage in prayer for self AND others. If you pray for others but neglect yourself, you have not finished your prayer. Remember, there are no first person singular pronouns in the Lord's teaching on prayer: It is OUR father; give US; forgive US; lead US; deliver US.

# EPILOGUE

P rayer is so misunderstood by the majority of Christians that we neglect its practice and fail to access its true power. I hope that this book has deepened your understanding of prayer and has stirred up in you a passion for expanding your personal relationship with God.

As we grow on this journey of prayer together, God is calling me to raise up an army or prayer warriors. I am fully convinced that when the church takes the Lord's teaching on prayer seriously, we will be able to bring about major positive and powerful change to our world. Building an army of prayer warriors begins by recruiting and training individuals.

I am recruiting you to join me in this battle for spiritual peace, prosperity and power. I am asking you to connect with me via social media so that we can hold each other accountable as we build a world-wide prayer ministry that brings about the healing of the nations. As we begin daily to be on one accord in prayer for self, family, church, community, country and world, our impact will be tremendous. Attitudes will begin to change and as a result, our actions will begin to change.

*I can be found on twitter at www.twitter.com/pastormikejones*
*I can be found on facebook at www.facebook.com/pastormj*

This type of corporate prayer, connecting believers around the world, will be one of the most positive forces for change that we have seen. God is calling His church to lead the world on our knees. Bear in mind that prayer is foundational to the process of change. After, we get serious in prayer; God will share more revelations and more opportunities for this massive prayer army to bring about real change in the real world. I hope that you will connect with me via social media (facebook, twitter, etc) so that we can worship together, work together, and win together for the Kingdom of God and the cause of Christ.

I love you with a pastor's heart and I am convinced that because of our connection to one another and to Christ, we will become world changers in ways that we never dreamed were possible. Grace and peace be unto you, your family, your community, your city, your country and this world. May the power of God and the life of Christ be manifest in you daily. AMEN!